The School of Nazareth

By Mark Hartfiel

PARADISUS DEI

PARADISUS DEI

P.O. Box 19127
Houston, TX 77224

www.paradisusdei.org

Cover Design: Allison Barrick
Original image by Iosif Chezan/Shutterstock.com

For my wife Katie, and my daughters Maria, Clare and Lucy

Table of Contents

Introduction to The School of Nazareth

There is a beautiful tradition in the Church that St. Joseph lived on the Earth with Jesus and Mary for thirty years. Thirty years to adore the face of Our Lord and Savior, thirty years to contemplate the mystery of the Incarnation, and thirty years to be a true father. Joseph experienced a life that no man in history can parallel. Joseph knew Jesus and Mary intimately. Not only that, in many mysterious ways, he led them.

Over the next thirty days we will set out upon a journey with St. Joseph in honor of the thirty years he spent with Jesus and Mary. We will seek to know him more deeply so that he may teach us to listen to the "still, small voice" of God and how to respond to it. He will teach us to be men after God's own heart!

This book can be read anytime during the year, but the most optimal times would be the thirty days leading up to one of two feast days:

- St. Joseph, Husband of Mary: **Begin on February 16** to finish with the Entrustment to St. Joseph on March 19.
- St. Joseph the Worker: **Begin on April 1** to finish with the Entrustment to St. Joseph on May 1.

On a personal note, my personal reflection and contemplation on the mystery of St. Joseph has been developed for over ten years as a participant in the *That Man is You!* men's program and countless conversations with its founder, Steve Bollman. I, like thousands of others, am forever grateful for your tireless service in the vineyard of the Lord.

I offer special thanks to the entire Paradisus Dei staff who labor so graciously with hearts of servants. To my brother, Matt, who made this book much better in every way. To my parents who first taught me at "The School of Nazareth" with their unconditional love. And finally my wife, Katie! It is her love and prayers that continue to work miracles in my heart.

In Christ,
Mark Joseph Hartfiel

Forward

It's a common question in today's world: "Where are all of the good men?" In the work I do with young single women, it is a question I hear often. Where are the men of honor, purity and sacrifice? Where are the men who are willing to fight for their bride? While they may be difficult to find through social media, in the news or at the corner bar, I assure these women that, indeed, they are out there.

The world needs more Saint Josephs, just as it needs more Marys. The world needs individuals ready to display their heroism. They say that to have a child is to allow your heart to walk around outside your body. If this is true, then Mary and Joseph allowed their hearts to be nailed to a tree. They know love. These two saints want nothing more than to exchange their hearts for yours. If we let them, they will teach us to love in a way we didn't know was possible. That notion is what this journey is all about.

Every week, tens of thousands of men gather across the world for their local *That Man Is You!* program in their parish. These men are becoming better men, better fathers and better husbands. They aren't doing it alone. In the example of Saint Joseph, they follow the footsteps to the cross, and their hearts, their homes and their families are being transformed. Where are all the good men in the world? I believe they are out there, and I believe one of them is holding this book in his hands.

St. Joseph made his earthly living crafting beautiful work, and he spends his heavenly life doing the same. Will you allow St. Joseph the carpenter to work on your heart over the next thirty days? Will you allow him to carefully craft the details of the inner workings of your relationship with Christ? Will you be his handiwork, so he can offer you as a masterpiece for Christ? Will you be an answer to the world's hunger for good men?

As you journey for the next thirty days, we will keep you in prayer. Be generous, and God will not disappoint.

Katie Hartfiel
Catholic Author and National Speaker
Womaninlove.org

Section 1:

An Introduction to St. Joseph

"St. Joseph was chosen among all men, to be the protector and guardian of the Virgin Mother of God; the defender and foster-father of the Infant-God, and the only co-operator upon earth, the one confidant of the secret of God in the work of the redemption of mankind."

St. Bernard of Clairvaux

DAY 1

Chosen

From all generations
From all peoples,
From all men,
Joseph was chosen.

From the moment of the fall of Adam and Eve, humanity awaited a Savior. Expectations grew over thousands of years while all of creation held its breath anticipating salvation. Of course, God's imagination is capable of constructing an infinite number of ways to manifest his love for us. He could have come in a magnificent fashion, blinding the world with his infinite glory that we may begin to see clearly again. If I were God, that's how I would have done it! Instead, he made the radical choice to leave his throne in the heavens and break into human history over 2,000 years ago as an infant, placing himself in the care of a mere man and woman. God the Father entrusted God the Son to two humans, Mary and Joseph. He became dependent upon their "Yes" and upon their love and protection to accomplish his most beautiful plan for our salvation.

God did not **need** Mary and Joseph, but in his unfathomable wisdom and providence, he **chose** them to play an essential role, as he carried out his divine plan. God chose to rely upon them for the care of his only Son, our Lord Jesus Christ. He has chosen St. Joseph for us as well. In the next thrity days, you will discover the father and model that desires an invitation into your home and family.

Personal Reflection:
Each day, we will explore an aspect of St. Joseph and follow with a personal reflection to relate this to our own lives. The personal reflection is intended to be a spiritual challenge to help us examine our current lives and lead us into deeper communion with God. As we "look in the mirror" a bit, we may feel uncomfortable. You may feel tempted at times to say to yourself, "I'm not that holy,

I don't have heroic virtue and trust, and I don't even know what mission God has given to me." Self-reflection and examination of your own spiritual life is of great value if you want to grow in your faith. Place your hope in the Lord and never despair of your weakness or sinfulness.

God doesn't choose the qualified, he qualifies the chosen. And God is calling you.

From all generations,
From all peoples,
From all men,
You have been chosen.

He has chosen **you** for your wife. He has chosen **you** for your children. He has chosen **you** for your family. He has chosen **you** for your vocation. He could have done things in a different way, but instead he chose to rely upon **your** faith, **your** trust and **your** love. He chose **you** to play an integral role in the salvation of those in your care. You have an incredible dignity and responsibility before you.

You see, our God is as intimate as he is infinite. God understands your situation. He knows what you are going through. He understands the crosses that you carry in your life and the ins and outs of your relationships. Whether you are married or single, he understands your struggles, **and within them he has an incredible plan for you and you alone.** There may be times when those plans are confusing and you might ask if God picked the right man for the job. Just as God handpicked a carpenter for a singular role in the history of the world, God is calling you… and he is calling for a reason. In the words of St. Francis of Assisi, "Your life may be the only sermon some people hear today." He is calling you in your home, in your workplace, in your daily tasks. He will call, and he will qualify.

Mary said Yes.
Joseph said Yes.
What do you say?

Heavenly Father, as I begin this journey, give me the faith and trust I need to follow you. Give me the courage to say "Yes" to you today and everyday of my life.

St. Joseph – illuminate the darkness that shrouds your life. Pierce the silence that hides your wisdom. Amen.

Day 2

He Spoke Not a Word

We have all heard it said that "actions speak louder than words." In the case of St. Joseph, we have not a single spoken word recorded in all of Scripture. I understand humility, but if it were me, I would have bargained with God for at least something! Joseph accomplished everything the Lord asked from him while spending thirty years in the presence of the God-Man and the Immaculate Conception. Surely, he had more than a few stories to tell! Yet, we hear not a word...

Why would the Holy Spirit will the hiddenness and silence of St. Joseph in Scripture? Did the second greatest saint in heaven truly have nothing to say? In this light, could he really have been all that important? On the contrary, this silence should speak loudly to us. St. Joseph is the ultimate example of the famous teaching of St. Francis of Assisi, "Preach the gospel at all times, and when necessary, use words." Throughout this journey, we will enter into the mystery of St. Joseph and allow him to "preach the gospel" to us through his actions and even through his silence. **If we have the spiritual ears to hear it**, God wishes to teach us something profound through the silence of St. Joseph.

St. Joseph was content to be hidden because he was not all about himself. St. Joseph was all about God. He had no desire to be in the limelight, no desire to get in a word or two, no desire for attention and no desire to make himself known. Therefore, his example teaches us an incredibly valuable and absolutely essential element in the spiritual life...**It's not about ME!** From the very start, we learn from him the essential virtue of **humility**.

It is hard, if not impossible, to truly possess any other virtue, if we are lacking in humility. Simply put, the opposite of humility is pride. Within every sin committed, there is an element of pride at its core. In the words of St. Augustine, "It was pride that changed angels into devils; it is humility that makes men as angels." If our other virtues are filled with pride, then they aren't really authentic virtues at all. Over the next month, we will see the abstract idea of humility put on flesh through the example of this unassuming carpenter. We are just getting started. The more we become acquainted with him, the more we enter into the mystery, and as we do so, the hidden character of St. Joseph will begin to be revealed.

Personal Reflection:

As you set out along this journey, start by reflecting on your own life. First and foremost, there is a need to enter into daily silence. **God desires to speak to you with a still, small voice.** If there is no room for silence in your life, it becomes impossible to hear that voice. **Don't be afraid to waste time with God.** Ask St. Joseph to help you make time for daily silence, and ask him to teach you to listen for the subtle and gentle voice of the Lord.

Second, you must begin this journey with the desire to grow in humility. You must come to an understanding that, in turning our focus from within, we find what we seek! St. Joseph was a master of this concept. Let us pursue this great humility by once again looking to the advice of St. Augustine, "Do you wish to rise? Begin by descending. You plan a tower that will pierce the clouds? Lay first the foundation of humility."

Heavenly Father – give me the grace to desire a deeper relationship with you. Help me to hear your whisper amidst the noise of my life. May your word be a lamp unto my feet and a light unto my path.

St. Joseph – illuminate the darkness that shrouds your life. Pierce the silence that hides your wisdom. Amen.

Day 3

St. Joseph Our Model

"Let your life be free from love of money, and be content with what you have; for as it is said, 'I will never fail you nor forsake you.'"
Hebrews 13:5

It is well known that many men struggle with the art of comparison. For some of us, it is an innate tendency toward competition. For others, it can be a badgering subconscious desire to size up the next guy. However it manifests itself, the majority of men are driven by a need to out-play, out-perform and out-do the competition in order to feel successful and fulfilled.

For most of our marriage, my wife and I have done ministry work within an affluent parish community. While our career choices definitely imply that we are not in our fields for the money, we have been invited to rub elbows in more than a few mansions over the years. Although I am 100% dedicated to the work my wife and I have chosen, I must admit that *every once in a while,* temptation knocks on my heart. In those moments when I compare myself to others, I ask, "Am I providing sufficiently for my family?" When I begin to equate my financial successes with my value as a husband and father, a subsequent question arises: "Am I a failure?"

I am probably not the only man who has had these temptations occasionally whispered in his ear. Three of the four Gospels recount Satan's same temptation of Christ himself, as he offered Christ the power and luxuries of the world. The Lord countered Satan's empty promises by vowing to us that when we reject the love of money and success, he doesn't leave us with a void. Instead, he fills us with his very self. He promises, "I will never forsake you or abandon you." The honest truth is that many of us are slaves to comparison, but **Christ promises to set us free.**

Of course, there is a man who heroically lived this truth with an unshakable trust paired with an unprecedented mission. While there are other men out there who are competing against you, St. Joseph isn't one of them. Joseph unspeakably stands as an amazing example of sanctity and what it means to be a real man. When I humbly invited St. Joseph to be an active presence in my life, I found that he didn't make me feel like a failure. On the contrary, Joseph gently whispered, "Mark, let me show you a more exceptional way. Let me come into your heart and your home and bring peace." He doesn't go to work for me, pay the bills or take care of the kids, but I appreciate that he does **so much more!**

Joseph is a gentle and loving father, a man after God's own heart. He is the man we all want to be. I would venture to say that during your journey through this book, St. Joseph will bring about a deeper relationship with **you.** This is because Joseph wants nothing more than to deliver you to God the Father and the Son, Jesus Christ. St. Louis de Montfort calls Mary the shortest, quickest, easiest way to Jesus. St. Joseph shares in this very mission. Get to know the entire Holy Family, and expect your heart to be transformed!

Personal Reflection:

As you personally draw closer to the humble St. Joseph, you will likely discover his heroic sanctity. This sanctity may bring to light an even greater perspective on your weaknesses and selfishness. Remember those whom God has chosen before you and never despair.

Abraham lied and was too old. Sarah laughed at God's promises. Moses stuttered. David was an adulterer and accomplice to murder. Hosea's wife was a prostitute. Amos' only training was in the school of fig-tree pruning. Jacob was a liar. Solomon was too rich. Jeremiah was too young. Naomi was a widow. Noah got drunk. Jonah ran from God and got swallowed by a whale! Mariam was a gossip. Thomas doubted. Peter denied Christ three times. Paul was a murderer. So was Moses. Jesus was too poor. (Author unknown).

We all have issues, insecurities and sins. Ask God for his infinite mercy and for St. Joseph to guide you beyond your weaknesses.

Heavenly Father – Thank you for the gift of your mercy and forgiveness. Help me not to compare or evaluate my spiritual life or my dignity based upon the lives of others, but instead let me focus upon my relationship with you. You are my Father, and I am your son. Thank you for the gift and example of your servant, St. Joseph.

St. Joseph – illuminate the darkness that shrouds your life. Pierce the silence that hides your wisdom. Amen.

Section 2:

A Just Man before God

"Though thou hast recourse to many saints as thine intercessors, go specially to St. Joseph, for he has great power with God."
St. Teresa of Avila, Doctor of the Church; Spiritual Maxims #65

Day 4

A Man After God's Own Heart

King David was the only man named in Scripture as a "man after God's own heart." This title stands out, because King David was the center of quite a scandal in his time. Not only did he have an adulterous affair, but he also became an accomplice to murder in his efforts to hide his sin. As the story unfolded, God sent the Prophet Nathan, David repented, and for ages humanity has been blessed to read some of the most beautiful penitential passages in all of Scripture (see Psalm 51). David's life exemplified an incredible testimony to the truth of the famous words of St. Paul, "where sin increased, grace abounded all the more" (Romans 5:20).

God "raised up David to be their king; of whom he testified and said, 'I have found in David, the son of Jesse, a man after my heart, who will do all my will'" (Acts 13:22). As men of God, our hearts' mission must align with David's in pursuit of the heart of the Father. Our actions, decisions, prayer and daily comings and goings should gratify the Lord.

Although King David was the only man we find in Scripture named as such, it is safe to say that St. Joseph was a man after God's own heart. He was single-minded and whole-hearted in his desire to follow and do God's will no matter the consequence. Consider what the Holy Spirit reveals to us about St. Joseph in the Scriptures. On four different occasions, God's will was revealed to Joseph by means of an angel, and in each instance, Joseph responded with complete obedience.

> But as he considered this, behold, an angel of the Lord appeared to him in a dream, saying, "Joseph, son of David, do not fear to take Mary your wife, for that which is conceived in her is of the Holy Spirit; she will bear a son, and you shall call his name Jesus, for he will save his people from their sins. (Matthew 1:20)

> When Joseph woke from sleep, **he did as the angel of the Lord commanded him**; he took his wife, but knew

her not until she had borne a son; and he called his name Jesus. (Matthew 1:24-25)

Now when they had departed, behold, an angel of the Lord appeared to Joseph in a dream and said, "Rise, take the child and his mother, and flee to Egypt, and remain there till I tell you; for Herod is about to search for the child, to destroy him. And **he rose and took the child and his mother by night**, and departed to Egypt. (Matthew 2:13-14)

But when Herod died, behold, an angel of the Lord appeared in a dream to Joseph in Egypt, saying, "Rise, take the child and his mother, and go to the land of Israel, for those who sought the child's life are dead." And **he rose and took the child and his mother**, and went to the land of Israel." (Matthew 2:19-21)

But when he heard that Archelaus reigned over Judea in place of his father Herod, he was afraid to go there, and **being warned in a dream he withdrew to the district of Galilee**. And he went and dwelt in a city called Nazareth." (Matthew 2:22-23)

St. Joseph intently listened to the voice of God and acted upon it from the time he awoke. Each day, we can hear St. Joseph emphatically resound, "Yes!" to the Lord's call and will. In the heart of Joseph was a desire to adore the heart of God, and as a result, his deepest desires were satisfied. He was living proof of King David's promise that you must, "find your delight in the Lord, who will give you your heart's desire" (Psalm 27:5).

Personal Reflection:

The world is desperate for more men like St. Joseph, men after God's own heart. In order to be one yourself, you must lay down your will at his feet, proclaiming in your heart along with Mary and Joseph, "Let it be to me according to your word" (Luke 1:38).

Tomorrow, we will consider the obstacles we must overcome.

Heavenly Father - give me the grace and desire to become a man after your own heart. Help me follow your will and trust in your goodness. Thy kingdom come, thy will be done.

St. Joseph – make me a man after God's own heart. Amen.

Day 5

Do Whatever He Tells You

While Joseph spoke not a word in Scripture, Our Lady spoke merely a few. Her words were powerful, and her final words say it all: "Do whatever he tells you" (John 2:5). Mary spoke them to the chief steward at the Wedding Feast of Cana, and she perpetually speaks them to her children throughout human history. These are Mary's words for us, the best and only Christian advice we need. Most people make things very complex, but Mary makes it very simple. In a single sentence, she sums up the entire life of St. Joseph, a life she witnessed firsthand. I'm sure this sentence was the mantra of their entire lives, and we are blessed that this wisdom has been passed along to us.

Yesterday, we heard that King David was honorably named "a man after my heart, who will do all my will" (Acts 13: 22). What merited this response from God? Precisely as God says, he "will do all my will."

For David, this desire manifested itself as a desire to be in the presence of God. As the story unraveled we find that God's plans differed from David's as he had something else in store. Although it must have been incredibly difficult, King David obeyed. David's heart longed for action as he yearned to build a temple where God could reside amongst his people. He began the preparations that his son, Solomon, would one day complete. David lived with a growing hunger to encounter the living God.

Nearly a thousand years later, a man once again experienced this presence of God in an earth-shattering way through unshakable obedience. "Joseph, son of David, do not fear to take Mary your wife, for that which is conceived in her is of the Holy Spirit; she will bear a son, and you shall call his name Jesus, for he will save his people from their sins" (Matthew 1:20-21).

The very person of God in flesh came to dwell in his home, eat at his table and work by his side. St. Joseph became a man after God's own heart, as he gazed into the eyes of the child that he loved more than life. Joseph worked to feed his family, prayed to lead his family, longed to bring joy to his family and made decisions for the

21

good of his family. By simply loving the son entrusted to him, St. Joseph became a man after God's own heart.

Personal Reflection:

Jesus promises that "where two or three are gathered together in my name, there am I in the midst of them" (Mt. 18:20). **Jesus longs to make good on this promise in the daily rhythm of your home**. Just as Joseph was a man after the heart of his son, that very same son is present in the heart of **your** family. Joseph was the pioneer of Christian fatherhood as he fathered Christ. Make no mistake, he intercedes for you now that you may be a man after God's own heart, and that you won't miss the presence of God dwelling so clearly within the walls of your home.

St. Joseph not only carried out God's will – he did not hesitate. He did not have a passive role in the story of our salvation, and he did not have a passive personality. He may have been meek and humble of heart, but St. Joseph was a man of action.

How is God calling you in your life and how will you respond? Do you have the humility and faith to *do whatever he tells you?*

Heavenly Father, at times it is very hard for me to discern your voice.

I desire to do your will. Help me draw closer to you and remove the clutter from my life, so that I may hear when you call. May your still, small voice be like thunder to my heart. Speak Lord, for your servant is listening.

St. Joseph, make me a man after God's own heart. Amen.

Day 6

Sower and the Seed

Scripture tells us St. Joseph was "a just man before God," and we now understand through our reflection that he was also "a man after God's own heart." In short, Joseph was good soil that bore abundant fruit. Today, let us consider Christ's parable of the sower and the seed. It speaks of both St. Joseph and of ourselves.

The story of the sower and the seed is unique. By definition, every man fits into one of the four categories, but at the same time, most of us have experienced a little of each.

For today's reflection, let us listen to the words of Christ and contemplate the obstacles for becoming fertile soil:

Personal Reflection:
The sower goes out to sow the Word of God.

1) "Some seeds fell along the path, and the birds came and devoured them" (Matthew 13:4). Christ explains, "When any one hears the word of the kingdom and does not understand it, the Evil One comes and snatches away what was sown in his heart" (Matthew 13:19).

- Is your heart united to God?
- What are the obstacles/distractions from this?

2) "Other seeds fell on rocky ground, where they had not much soil, and immediately they sprang up, since they had no depth of soil, but when the sun rose they were scorched; and since they had no root they withered away" (Matthew 13:5-6). Christ explains, "As for what was sown on rocky ground, this is he who hears the word and immediately receives it with joy; yet he has no root in himself, but endures for awhile and when tribulation or persecution arises on account of the word, immediately he falls away" (Matthew 13:20-21).

- Are you rooted in Christ or in the comforts of the world?
- What is the evidence of this in your daily routine?

3) "Other seeds fell upon thorns, and the thorns grew up and choked them" (Matthew 13:7). Christ explains, "This is he who hears the word, but the cares of the world and the delight in riches choke the word, and it proves unfruitful" (Matthew 13:22).

- Is your **ultimate** desire for worldly success or to serve the Lord?
- What desires choke the Word in your personal life?

4) "Other seeds fell on good soil and brought forth grain, some a hundredfold, some sixty, some thirty" (Matthew 13:8). Christ explains, "This is he who hears the word and understands it; he indeed bears fruit, and yields, in one case a hundredfold, in another sixty, and in another thirty" (Matthew 13:23).

- Are you like Joseph? Do you listen to God's word, understand it, and rise up to fulfill it?
- How does it change your life when you accomplish the will of the Father?

Heavenly Father - help me to set aside the distractions in my life, so that I may become the good soil. Help me detach myself from my own disordered passions that cause me to lose the seed that you have planted within my soul. Help me to listen, to understand, and to do your will. Use me to bear great fruit. Make me more like St. Joseph. Amen.

St. Joseph – make me a man after God's own heart. Amen.

Day 7

Total Abandonment

The Lord can accomplish marvels through souls who abandon themselves completely to his will! Abandonment, properly understood, includes a full and total gift of self. We give everything. It requires heroic humility, deep interior faith, unshakable confidence and radical obedience. The irony is that in abandonment, we find perfect fulfillment of our greatest desires. When we lose ourselves, we find ourselves.

As men, we often feel a duty to "man the ship", so to speak. We naturally lead, guide and protect. Perhaps the responsibility is at times overbearing. We can regularly feel as if so many people depend on us to steer them with all the right answers. While we often times bear the obligation to be the compass for other people, abandonment can sound unpractical and unachievable.

Ironically, Saint Therese insisted, "It is abandonment alone which guides me. I have no other compass" (Manuscrits Autobiographiques, 207). As her spirituality matured, St. Therese found that she was no longer driven by her own desires. The two competing compasses of her past had been reduced to one: doing the will of God. In our lives, jobs and families, there is only one person who should be steering the ship, and we should follow his every order. When God finds souls like St. Therese, he is free to accomplish whatever he wills through them. Pause for a moment to consider: what would life be like if you surrendered everything, and I mean **everything**, to the Lord?

We cannot know for certain, but I believe Joseph possessed heroic virtues and sanctity long before he knew of his historical vocation. Joseph had long before united his own will to the will of God. Therefore, God knew there was an open vessel to carry out his most beautiful plan for the salvation of souls.

When we abandon our lives to the will of God, no matter what happens, **we experience a profound inner peace**. St. Joseph's very life was a testament to this reality. Reflect on the events surrounding the birth of Christ and his infancy. The Holy Family fled on a donkey to a town called Bethlehem and could not find a room to sleep. I don't know many women who would be thrilled to be nine months pregnant, about to go into labor and be forced to sleep outside. Imagine telling your bride, "Don't worry, dear! We can lay down our newborn in this feeding trough after the birth."

Things did not get any easier after the birth. King Herod was infuriated that he had been tricked by the wise men and decided that the only way to ensure his reign continued would be to have all the males under the age of two killed (Matthew 2:16). The infamous Massacre of the Innocents is hard to imagine even 2,000 years later. Joseph fled Israel and had his wife and child on the run once again. In obedience, they went to Egypt, where they waited for further instruction from the angel of the Lord. After Herod's death, he took his family back to Israel, but then was forced to withdraw to the district of Galilee and finally to the small, obscure town of Nazareth. God's plans for Joseph didn't always make sense, but as long as the Lord was at the helm, Joseph knew he was on the right track.

Through Joseph's journey, a profound peace was born from the fruit of trust, obedience and abandonment to the will of God. The peace in the hearts of Mary and Joseph did not remain internal and invisible but became physical and tangible. The Peace of God was born and laid in swaddling clothes in that manger. Both angels and animals were present before the one who was both God and man. The spiritual and the physical became incarnate in the Christ-child. **There was a cosmic harmony the Earth had not yet experienced until that silent night.** Peace was present in the midst of what the rest of the world would call chaos. That is what Joseph and the Holy Family experienced. St. Paul described it as peace "which surpasses all understanding" (Philippians 4:7).

God had a plan, and his will was accomplished. To see it through, he chose a man after his own heart. Peace entered the world through abandonment.

Personal Reflection:

Christ proclaimed to the disciples, "My food is to do the will of him who sent me, and to accomplish his work" (John 4:34). Do you trust in the goodness of God enough to lay your life down in abandonment to his will? What is holding you back? Fear of suffering? Fear of failure? Fear you will miss out on all the fun? Do not worry if you are weak, for God promises, "My grace is sufficient for you, for my power is made perfect in weakness" (2 Corinthians 12:9). "Confidence is perfected in worry, humility is perfected in the movements of pride, light is perfected in darkness" (Father Jean d'Elbee, *I Believe in Love*).

It comes down to believing and trusting in the goodness of God and then having the humility to believe that he loves **you**. He longs to fulfill his plans for your life. As surely as he did for St. Joseph, he longs to bring peace into your life.

Heavenly Father – ease the doubts, fears, and distractions that cloud my mind and my heart. Help me to take another step in my spiritual life by laying all that I have and all that I am at your feet. Jesus, I trust in you!

St. Joseph – make me a man after God's own heart. Amen.

Section 3:

The Spouse of Mary

"But as he considered this, behold, an angel of the Lord appeared to him in a dream, saying, 'Joseph, son of David, do not fear to take Mary your wife, for that which is conceived in her is of the Holy Spirit; she will bear a son, and you shall call his name Jesus, for he will save his people from their sins.' All this took place to fulfill what the Lord had spoken by the prophet: 'Behold, a virgin shall conceive and bear a son, and his name shall be called Emmanuel' (which means, God with us).

When Joseph woke from sleep, he did as the angel of the Lord commanded him; he took his wife, but knew her not until she had borne a son; and he called his name Jesus."
Matthew 1:20-25

Day 8

Unprecedented Event

You are at a party, maybe a couple's shower or wedding that your wife insisted you attend, while your favorite sports team is playing in a pivotal game. Your DVR is set, and you anxiously await the chance to get home to watch everything play out. Suddenly, another unwilling male attendee loudly announces the final score of the game that you are looking forward to watching in its entirety. How does this change the way you perceive the drama and play-by-play of the game later? Does knowing the end change the way you experience it? Unfortunately, this is how we read the Scriptures. We know what comes next, and how the Old Testament ends with the anticipation and coming of the Savior! We must try to remember that these characters had no idea how things would unfold. The magnitude of Joseph's reaction to Mary's pregnancy can be easily lost in our awareness that everything turns out fine in the end.

Try to place yourself in Joseph's shoes. If your fiancée had just informed you that she was pregnant by way of the Holy Spirit, your emotions would most likely be filled with betrayal, fury and heartbreak.

St. Joseph was a much calmer and wiser man, as you can imagine. He did not respond in this way. He struggled with how he would handle this situation. In the midst of his struggle, God sent an angel to explain to him that what Mary said was true. The angel explained there was nothing to fear and that he should take her as his wife. Joseph arose and did what the angel asked of him.

This was truly an unprecedented event in human history. Even though St. Joseph had great faith, there was no previous example of God working in this way before. His quick response showed his confidence that God was capable of doing the impossible. At the core of his being resided unshakeable faith that God was a God of miracles. Joseph was utterly confident in the fact that God was alive and active, both in the creation of the world and the daily lives of each and every soul he so masterfully created. St. Joseph believed that God dynamically intervenes in human history and was humble enough to surrender to God's plan.

God could have made the decision easier for Mary and Joseph. When he sent Gabriel to Mary, Joseph was not present. Therefore, Mary's *fiat* (her Yes!) was made independent of Joseph. She had no idea how he would respond when finding out about her miraculous pregnancy! Her *fiat* demonstrated her unwavering faith in God and her outright trust in Joseph. It was only after Mary told Joseph what had taken place that God sent an angel to Joseph. God relied on their personal decisions to trust in **him** and in **one another** before sharing the details of his plan with Joseph.

Through the experience from this unprecedented event, I have no doubt that Mary and Joseph learned to trust in God more than ever. For Mary, she would hold on to this immovable faith and trust all the way to the foot of the cross. They knew God was in control. No matter how it appeared to the rest of the world, they knew God had a plan.

Their example teaches us something about God as well as something about both Mary and Joseph. Their faith in God was unshakeable. Their trust in his plan was unfailing. Joseph would follow God's will at all costs, no matter what it meant for his own life. When I think about this obedience, I can't help but think about Christ himself. Like father, like son.

Personal Reflection:

God seeks men of faith. God can move mountains in your life and the lives of others if he finds in you the faith of a mere mustard seed. Jesus reminds us, "All things are possible to him who believes" (Mark 9:23). In difficult moments, when you do not understand and your faith is tested, remember that God's ways are not your ways, and his thoughts are not your thoughts. His plans are infinitely higher. It is in these moments in particular that you must place your life and the lives of your loved ones in his hands. Allow St. Joseph to be your guide.

Heavenly Father – inspire in me a faith like St. Joseph's, so that I may always trust in your ways.

St. Joseph – unveil for me the love of the Holy Spirit present in my spouse. Amen.

Day 9

Decided to Divorce Her Quietly

Yesterday, we considered the news proclaimed in the Annunciation to both Mary and Joseph as an unprecedented event in human history. We came to a deeper appreciation of the heroic faith of Mary **and** Joseph. However, in this consideration, we skipped over a monumental detail. Namely, after Mary broke the news, but before God sent an angel to speak to Joseph in his dream, there was a serious dilemma to discern.

Joseph, being a just man and unwilling to put her to shame, resolved to divorce her quietly. (Matthew 1:19)

At first glance, this phrase from Scripture makes little sense. It seems to contradict itself, in that a just man would choose divorce. If Joseph understood the baby to be from God, then he should naturally conclude that Mary had no shame. But Joseph was living in a different era and culture than today. According to the Mosaic Law, if a woman who was married or betrothed was found guilty of an adulterous affair, she would be taken outside the city gates and stoned to death (Deuteronomy 2:23). Even though he did not fully understand the situation at this point in time, having Mary stoned to death was not a viable option for Joseph. Therefore, he decided to "divorce her quietly," so that no one would know he was not responsible for this pregnancy. Instead, Joseph accepted that, over time, the town would have noticed that Mary was pregnant and assumed the baby was Joseph's. Mary would have been safe from stoning, but the people of Nazareth would have assumed that Joseph selfishly and dishonorably left Mary and her child on their own to fend for themselves.

Joseph was willing to take this apparent "shame" of Mary upon his own shoulders. Risking his reputation, Joseph once again pointed to Christ. Jesus became the victim of the greatest injustice in all of humanity. Indeed, it was our shame that he took upon **his** shoulders when he carried his cross to Calvary. Christ was willing to be ridiculed and convicted of a crime he did not commit **so that we may be set free**.

Christ taught us that his actions reflected those of the Father (John 5:19). While Jesus was referring to God the Father, it is apparent that his heavenly father chose for his son an earthly father who taught him mercy and sacrifice as well.

Personal Reflection:

Ponder the limitless mercy of God in your own life and, in turn, how merciful you are to others. Once you receive the mercy of God, you are called to be an instrument of that mercy to the world. If you are married, ask St. Joseph to teach you how to be merciful to your bride, just as he was to Mary. St. Joseph was placed in a seemingly impossible situation, and yet he still chose mercy. Why? How? The explanation for Joseph's courageous and noble actions is humility, which is precisely why we began this book with that virtue. St. Joseph understood that it's not about himself. He understood that his life was an offering for others, and that you only truly find yourself when you give yourself away. St. Joseph was already living the Christian way of mercy before Christianity even existed. He was a herald to a new Way.

Heavenly Father, shower your mercy upon me, so that I may be a man like St. Joseph and offer my life in sacrifice for others.

St. Joseph – unveil for me the love of the Holy Spirit present in my spouse. Amen.

Day 10

Most Chaste Spouse

St. Paul sets before husbands the standard in which they are called to love their wives:

> Husbands, love your wives, as Christ loved the Church and gave himself up for her...that he might present the church to himself in splendor, without spot or wrinkle or any such thing. (Ephesians 5: 25, 27)

St. Joseph has many titles in Catholic tradition, including "Most Chaste Spouse." This truth is highlighted in the second Marian Dogma as it describes deep truths about Mary. The Church teaches that Mary maintained "perpetual virginity" as she remained a virgin before, during and after the birth of Christ. Practically speaking, her perpetual virginity meant that Mary and Joseph did not have sexual relations.

Now, let's be cautious with the implications of this statement. First and foremost, this does not mean that union between a man and woman in the context of marriage is in any way wrong or sinful. In fact, quite the opposite is true. We have been blessed, especially through the teachings of St. John Paul II, to know that the sexual union between spouses in marriage is in fact holy. When we cooperate with God in this way, we become co-creators with him, and through our love, we bring about new life to the world. Our love and our union are called to bear fruit. Beautiful!

For spouses, the physical union is an outward sign of the invisible union of their love for one another. Our love binds us together as one in Holy Matrimony. So why would Mary and Joseph refrain from such a holy, physical union? It is a deep mystery, but God has chosen to highlight the **spiritual union** of their marriage rather than the physical. In his providence, God destined Mary to be the New Eve, the Mother of all of humanity in the order of grace. In this way, she is our spiritual mother. Eve is our mother according to the flesh, and Mary is our mother according to the spirit. **God**

willed to highlight through the marriage of Mary and Joseph that we are more than just flesh! We are more than just physical beings! The union between man and woman is much deeper than a physical union. The physical union is a sign, a sacrament of the deeper, spiritual union. Mary and Joseph exemplified this spiritual union and help point us to a deeper meaning of marriage. Although their union was not a physical one, it was indeed exceptionally fruitful. Life himself came into the world through Mary and gave us the true fruit from the Tree of Life by sustaining us with his flesh and blood in the Eucharist.

Joseph lived St. Paul's mandate to the Ephesians to the fullest. He loved Mary with all of his heart. He helped ensure that her immaculate flesh remained totally for Our Lord. As the first tabernacle of Jesus Christ, our Blessed Mother contained the holiest of holies, and Joseph played an active role in safeguarding that purity.

Personal Reflection:

Reflect on the passage from Ephesians 5 and the purity of St. Joseph. God gave you the gift of your sexuality to be given away to your spouse but certainly not to be abused. Remember that your body and the body of your spouse are ultimately the Lord's. We are called to be a temple of God where his Spirit dwells. If you are married, treat your spouse with the dignity she deserves in all aspects of your marriage, so that when that final days comes, you can joyfully meet the Lord and *present her without spot or wrinkle or any such thing.*

Heavenly Father, thank you for the gift of sexuality and the pleasure that comes with it. Teach me to love my bride as you love the Church, and help me to preserve her dignity and purity. Guide me in the ways of St. Joseph, always putting the needs of others over my own desires.

St. Joseph – unveil for me the love of the Holy Spirit present in my spouse. Amen.

Day 11

The Immaculata

"[Mary] is the one whom every man loves when he loves a woman—whether he knows it or not. She is what every woman wants to be when she looks at herself. She is the woman whom every man marries in ideal when he takes a spouse; she is hidden as an ideal in the discontent of every woman with the carnal aggressiveness of man; she is the secret desire every woman has to be honored and fostered; she is the way every woman wants to command respect and love because of the beauty of her goodness of body and soul. And this blueprint love, whom God loved before the world was made, this Dream Woman before women were, is the one of whom every heart can say in its depth of depths: 'She is the woman I love!'" (Archbishop Fulton Sheen, The World's First Love)

In this segment of our journey, we are considering St. Joseph's role as spouse of Mary. In order to fully appreciate this unique vocation, we shall take a moment to consider who Mary is. Thousands of books are written about the Blessed Mother without exhausting her singular dignity. Therefore, the next few paragraphs will provide but a small taste of the beauty of our Blessed Mother.

Full of Grace

"Hail, full of grace, the Lord is with you." Luke 1:28

The superabundant mercy of God not only forgives sin but it also precedes the soul, so that we will not fall into sin in the first place. It is always our choice to receive or reject that mercy. In his divine providence, Mary received this superabundant mercy and fullness of God's grace from the moment of her Immaculate Conception. For this reason, she would never fall into sin at any moment of her life. Eve was given extraordinary grace as well, but where Eve is known for her "No," Mary is known for her resounding "Yes!"

Spouse of the Spirit

"The Holy Spirit will come upon you, and the power of the Most High will overshadow you." Luke 1:35

Thanks to her openness and faithfulness, the Holy Spirit filled the life and soul of Mary. St. Maximilian Kolbe, the greatest of Marian theologians, would go so far as to say she was, in fact, "the spouse of the Holy Spirit." We know that Mary is not God without an ounce of divinity in her; nonetheless, the union between Mary and the Holy Spirit is unparalleled and unmistakable. Mary was so completely docile to the actions of the Holy Spirit in her life that she always said yes to his movement. When you behold Mary move or speak, you are witnessing the manifestation of her union with the Holy Spirit.

Living Tabernacle

"Blessed are you among women, and blessed is the fruit of your womb." Luke 1:42

In the Old Testament, the presence of God dwelled in the temple where the Ark of the Covenant was kept. However, it wasn't so easy to gain access to the presence of God. One must go past the outer courts, into the center of the temple, to find the Ark in the Holiest of Holies. In fact, only a Levitical Priest could enter into these inner courts where the Ark was kept. What made the Ark holy was the fact that it contained the Ten Commandments and the Mosaic Covenant with Israel. As such, the presence of God dwelt above the Holy of Holies.

The Old Testament signs are brought into New Testament realities in numerous ways. Jesus Christ becomes the *Lamb of God*, slain for our sins and those of the whole world to save us and restore us to new life. Likewise, the God of the universe no longer dwelt in a physical sanctuary, but brought his presence to humanity in a new way: as a child born from a woman. Mary becomes the New Testament fulfillment as the living Ark. God is holy, holy, holy and literally dwelt in her womb. Mary was a living, breathing tabernacle of the Lord for nine months. She gave birth to the Author of Life!

Spouse of Joseph

God created Mary as his masterpiece to be a fitting vessel to carry the Word Incarnate in her womb, to nurse him, to care for him, to love him and to be by his side until the very end. God now needed a man that was fit to be the spouse of his masterpiece. He chose Joseph. Joseph was given the dignity of being her spouse, to love and honor her all the days of his life, and to keep her pure and holy.

If you have read my wife's book, *Woman In Love*, then you know the story of her praying for her future husband for years before she even met him. She prayed intensely for God to convert holy men into the world. Although we had never met and lived in different states, my sudden conversion came the exact week that she made a passionate resolve to journal to God with this intention. She wrote hundreds of letters to her "Husband-to-Be" (her HTB) and presented them to me the night before we exchanged our vows. What a way to start a marriage! Sometimes when we tell our story, people tell me, "Wow, what pressure you have to live up to that! She prayed for you all those years."

Pressure? Imagine St. Joseph! His wife was the Blessed Virgin Mary!

> When a man loves a woman, he has to become worthy of her. The higher her virtue, the more noble her character, the more devoted she is to truth, justice, goodness, the more a man has to aspire to be worthy of her. (Fulton J. Sheen, *Life is Worth Living*)

Personal Reflection:

Mary personifies the standard for what it means to be fully woman. She possesses true feminine genius. Mary was holy, and she sheds light on genuine womanhood. As a man, you are called to treat each woman, especially your spouse, with dignity befitting of God's masterpiece. The objectification of women in our culture is a great tragedy. You must not allow the world to distort your vision of women. Instead, allow St. Joseph to teach you to view women as he did. The devil is an imposter and, in his cunning ways, has tricked modern man to exchange love for lust. As Christians, we can do better. "It is the duty of every man to uphold the dignity of every woman" (Pope John Paul II, General Audience, November 24, 1982).

Heavenly Father, thank you for the gift of Our Lady and for the gift of my spouse. Help me grow in purity of heart and mind in all my relationships. Inspire me to never objectify others, but rather to honor the beauty and sanctity of women and without fail uphold their dignity and virtue.

St. Joseph, unveil for me the love of the Holy Spirit present in my spouse. Amen.

Day 12

Spouse of Our Lady of Sorrows

Do you ever notice particular lines from a song that strike you so deeply that you will never forget them? One such line for me comes from the band MercyMe and their song, "Bring The Rain." The song begins,

I can count a million times
People asking me how I
Can praise You with all that I've gone through.
The question just amazes me.
Can circumstances possibly
Change who I forever am in You?

For many of us, the circumstances that life brings can oftentimes take away our peace. If we allow it, difficult situations can diminish our joy and even lead us into despair. The song lyrics above bring such amazing clarity and truth! **We cannot allow the storms of this life to rob us of our joy**, but in our trials trust in the Lord as he promises, "The joy of the Lord will be my strength" (Nehemiah 8:10).

This recalls to mind a story of one of my close friend's father. Michael Morton was wrongly incarcerated in the 1980s for the brutal murder of his wife. He lost his spouse, his three year-old son, and his freedom for the next quarter century. Moreover, practically everyone he had ever known or loved presumed he was guilty. In prison, this man went through all the emotions of anger and hatred, but several years into his sentence he had a radical conversion. As he grew in his relationship with the Lord, he came to an understanding that even if he never got out of prison, he was content with his life. Why? How? Because he came to understand in the depths of his being that:

1) God is real.
2) God is wise.
3) God loves him.

Mr. Morton says in the documentary, *An Unreal Dream*, "If you understand these three things, what is your problem?" Twenty-five years after entering prison in the most miraculous of circumstances, Michael Morton was finally vindicated and exonerated of all charges. DNA testing had proved his innocence and life in prison was no longer. He was set free! I have seen him dozens of times, and he is never without a smile. He literally radiates joy. My good friend, now an adult, was the three year-old who lost his mother to murder and his father to prison. He, too, has found the Lord and lives with great joy.

I have heard more than a few priests talk about the three rings of marriage. The bride's ring, the groom's ring, and suffer-ring. When Mary and Joseph brought their newborn son to the temple, a new concern was brought to their attention. Simeon prophesized to Mary, "Your heart will be pierced by a sword" (Luke 2:35). Can you imagine what it would feel like to hear that your wife's heart will be pierced by a sword? From a human perspective, that news would certainly leave you uneasy, whether you are a saint or not. I, for one, would probably think it about and worry about it every moment of every day. Spouses take on the pain of their beloved even more than if it were their own!

Sometimes we are tempted to think that the Holy Family just had it easy and that the circumstances of their life must have been so peaceful. The truth is that the storms surrounding their lives were an all-out war. From the very beginning, Herod tried to kill their child, and we all know how the story ended 33 years later.

How could Joseph and Mary live with joy under these difficult circumstances in life? The joy of the Lord was their strength!

St. Joseph lived with Jesus for approximately thirty years on this earth. He came to a deep understanding, just like Bart Millard of MercyMe and Michael Morton, that circumstances cannot possibly change who he was in the heart and mind of God. This truth prevailed over any and every circumstance of life...even knowing that a sword would soon pierce the heart of his spouse.

"Bring the Rain" continues:

> *I am Yours regardless of*
> *The dark clouds that may loom above,*
> *Because You are much greater than my pain.*

You who made a way for me
By suffering Your destiny,
So tell me: what's a little rain?

Personal Reflection:

Difficult things have happened in the past, and you can worry about what is to come in the future. However, if you live with Jesus in the present moment, he will give you a peace and joy that surpasses all understanding (Philippians 4:7). That is his promise. It won't always be easy, but he will always be with you. If you lose sight of him, desperation may come but if you stay close to him and truly intimate with him like St. Joseph, then **he will be your strength** even in the midst of your weakness. It's precisely when we are weak that he is strong (Cf. 2 Corinthians 12:10).

- When have your circumstances led you to a crisis of faith?
- When has the Lord given you a peace and joy that surpasses all understanding?
- How can you begin living a foretaste of paradise today?

Heavenly Father, help me to seek union with you through each day of my life. If I find that our union is lacking, may that be my reminder to unite myself to you once more. I lay all of my burdens at your feet. May your grace be sufficient. Help me to continue to live a life of peace and joy no matter what storms come my way. Give me the radical faith and trust to allow you to remain asleep in the boat while a storm raged! If I ever find myself sinking in the darkness of the night, I will call out your name, and you will calm my distress. Father, I lift up to you all those who have very heavy crosses to bear in this life. Run to them, Lord, and be their Prince of Peace. Restore them to your joy. In their weakness, be their strength.

St. Joseph, unveil for me the love of the Holy Spirit present in my spouse. Amen.

Day 13

Pure of Heart

Oftentimes it is life's greatest blessings that we take for granted. Rarely do we think about our heart's ability to beat, our brainwaves directing every thought and action or our lungs filling with air. We surely would notice immediately should any of these functions be taken away! One of these faculties that many live without is the ability to see. It is hard to fathom never having seen a sunset, a child's face or a breathtaking cathedral. However, not only is this gift of sight often overlooked, it can even be used for evil. This shameful reality gives power to Jesus' statement, "If your eye causes you to sin, pluck it out and throw it away; it is better for you to enter life with one eye than with two eyes to be thrown into the hell of fire" (Matthew 18:9).

In the spiritual life, sin is a cause for blindness. In a very real and terrifying way, sin affects our ability to see, know and understand principles of our faith. Sin clouds our vision by darkening the intellect and weakening the will. A darkened intellect results in the inability to comprehend the truths of our faith. As St. John tells us, "the light shines in the darkness, and the darkness cannot comprehend it" (John 1:5). A weakened will makes us prone to further sin. It is easy to see how this path leads us further away from God and deeper into frustration. Eventually, we can become blind to the truth, as we wonder why we cannot hear, feel or see the work of God in our own personal lives.

However, many of us can say, "I was blind but now I see." Light overcomes the darkness, and purity overcomes sinfulness. **Where purity abides, clarity thrives.** It is only through this purity of heart that one can truly see. Jesus proclaims, "Blessed are the pure of heart, for they shall see God" (Matthew 5: 8). Truly, St. Joseph looked upon the face of God every day for thirty years. Joseph personifies the model of purity, of true vision and clarity. They say that the eye is the window to the soul, but it works in the opposite direction as well. Purity of heart allows the soul to bring light to all that surrounds us.

Enveloped by a world bombarded with impurity, it is clear why many feel that God has gone silent. Some ask if God has forgotten us, or if he was ever there to begin with. On the other hand, many witness a magnificent sunrise or face of a child and find themselves moved with conviction stating emphatically, "How could anyone not believe in God? They must be blind."

Personal Reflection:

Imagine how Christ rubbed the eyes of the blind man, and as his eyes were opened, the first sight he ever saw was the face of the Savior. Now recall the times in your own life when you were blinded by your own sinfulness and how Christ came to set you free. Christ longs to show you his face. He longs to heal you from anything that is blocking or distorting your image of him. The surest path is your purity. In our day, purity takes effort because the Devil never sleeps. Temptation is right around the corner. Maybe even more appropriately stated for modern times, **temptation is always one click away**.

Christ taught us "every one who commits sin is a slave to sin" (John 8:34). Allow him to set you free, and you will see the world with a new perspective.

Heavenly Father, the deepest desire of my heart is to see your face. Nothing else will satisfy. Help me strive towards an authentic purity of heart in all of my thoughts and actions. Like St. Joseph, help me see your hand and hear your voice so that I may follow you wherever you lead me.

St. Joseph, unveil for me the love of the Holy Spirit present in my spouse. Amen.

Day 14

Through Her and In Her

Some say that you don't understand the love of God until you become a parent. On June 25, 2008, we experienced the birth of our first daughter. There is no doubt that my heart soared like an eagle that day. As I embraced my newfound fatherhood more and more that first year of Maria's life, I felt as if I had a completely new understanding and connection to God the Father. If I, a sinful man, could look over my sleeping child's bed with a tidal wave of love in my heart, how much more must God the Father love his children? Could it be possible? My human brain cannot even comprehend the depths of such an intense and divine love. One of the greatest gifts the Lord has given us is the gift of fatherhood.

Today is our final day of reflection on Joseph, Spouse of Mary. As we contemplate, it makes sense to bridge this topic with the next: Joseph, Father of Jesus. This gift and dignity that God gives each of us as fathers can only happen in and through our spouse! It's a very simple truth that is so easily forgotten. We miss it daily. Even when we are conscious enough to thank God for our children, do we thank our spouse? She is the one that gives us our fatherhood. It is only through her that this is possible. She is the vessel in which God awards man with his greatest dignity!

St. Joseph sheds even more light and clarity on this reality. In the mind and heart of Joseph, this truth was even more glaring as he was not the biological father of Jesus. Joseph's child was not the conception of love between he and his spouse. His child, and therefore his fatherhood, came as a pure gift from the Holy Spirit and Mary. It was the work of God cooperating with the most vulnerable "Yes" in human history. With such a miraculous conception, there is no question that Joseph understood exactly where his fatherhood came from and hence where he owed his deepest gratitude.

Personal Reflection:

Imagine a world in which all husbands adored their children and spouses and went to great lengths to express their love and affection for them. Imagine a world with more men like St. Joseph!

For part one of your examination of conscience today, if you are a father, reflect on how well you have cherished the gift of fatherhood. I have no doubt Joseph considered his earthly fatherhood of the Christ-child to be both his greatest dignity and greatest gift from God.

For part two of your examination of conscience, ponder whether or not your spouse understands the depths of gratitude you have for her in giving you the gift of your fatherhood. Make a resolution today to affirm with her that she has given you the greatest gift. Convey to her the dignity that she deserves. Thank her for her vulnerability. A woman will tell you that her life is flipped upside down when she gets pregnant, especially for the first time. Everything changes. She needs to know what that gift of herself means to you.

Ask St. Joseph to show you the secrets of his heart and therefore set yours ablaze with the love and gratitude for your bride. Ask him to help you love your spouse as he loved Mary.

Heavenly Father, help me to always be thankful for the gift of my spouse. Help me to honor and cherish her all the days of my life. Thank you for bringing us together in your providence.

St. Joseph, unveil for me the love of the Holy Spirit present in my spouse. Amen.

Section 4:

The Father of Jesus

"The admirable St. Joseph was given to the earth to express the adorable perfection of God the Father in a tangible way. In his person alone, he bore the beauties of God the Father ... one saint alone is destined to represent God the Father."
Fr. Andrew Doze, The Shadow of the Father

"Behold, I will send you Elijah the prophet before the great and terrible day of the Lord comes. And he will turn the hearts of fathers to their children and the hearts of children to their fathers, lest I come and smite the land with a curse."
Malachi 4:6

Day 15

The Heart of a Father

The summer before my freshman year of college, everything changed for me. It was then that I had my first authentic, life-altering encounter with the living God. Having tasted this goodness there was no going back. As I entered into my first few years at a state school, I began to dive deeper into the theology of the Catholic Church and my hunger for the fullness of truth only seemed to grow. By the end of my sophomore year, I was spending more time listening to audiocassette tapes about the faith and reading Dr. Scott Hahn books than I was applying to my finance degree. Through this experience, I felt God calling me to transfer to Franciscan University of Steubenville and earn some college credits for those theology studies!

Upon arriving at Franciscan, my heart came alive as it was exposed to even more opportunities for growth. This being said, as a typical young man in college, it was easy to fall in love. Love was in the air at Steubenville, and I fell head over heels in love with none other than St. Therese of Lisieux. Don't worry, you can tell my wife. She knows all about it! I'm actually pretty sure Therese is the one who introduced me to my wife, Katie, but that is another story. During this first year at Franciscan, I was introduced to a work on St. Therese that remains my favorite spiritual book, *I Believe in Love*, by Fr. Jean C. J. d'Elbée. It's the only book that I have read close to a dozen times. I have no doubt that God placed Therese in my path intentionally, but it would take several more years for me to fully understand the Lord's master plan.

As the story continues, Katie and I got married and named our first child after my favorite saint – Maria Therese. Through her birth, God promptly placed a new favorite in my path, St. Louis Martin, the father of St. Therese. After reading the book, *The Father of the Little Flower*, I was stunned to discover that the vast majority of the spiritual gems I loved in St. Therese actually originated from her father! St. Therese has been acclaimed "the greatest saint of modern times," precisely because many believe she is the one who understood most simply and most profoundly the fatherhood of

God. Her vision of God the Father was shaped by daily witness of her earthly father. St. John Paul II beautifully proclaimed that men relive and reveal on earth the very fatherhood of God (Cf. Familiaris Consortio). St. Louis Martin had five daughters and every one of them became a nun. I knew then that the Lord introduced me to St. Therese in order for her to introduce me to her father. He was teaching me my ultimate mission in life – to be a father and, with his grace, to help form souls for heaven.

I dare say St. Louis Martin would have never been known in my life or in the life of the Church had it not been for his daughter Therese. The same can be said about St. Joseph. The sanctity of the child enlightened us in hindsight about the father. Both Louis Martin and Joseph lived their lives in service to the mission and vocation that God handed them; namely their children. They were both willing to go unnoticed in the world and lay down their personal ambitions. **The heart of a father beats for his children.** As fathers, what greater legacy can we possibly dream of than this?

Personal Reflection

It is easy to get wrapped up in the cares and trappings of the world and be tempted to identify ourselves with our achievements. In heaven, no one will care about your earthly bank account, home or popularity. Your life will not be judged by your worldly success, but based on your personal sanctity and extent at which you helped lead other souls to heaven. We know St. Joseph and St. Louis Martin in light of their children. You can become a great saint, known or unknown does not matter, if you are willing to help form your children into saints. Lead them to God by your words and all your actions every single day. Parents are the primary and most influential teachers of the faith to their children.

- Are you raising your children to become saints?
- Do you teach your children that pleasing God is more important than pleasing the world?
- In what ways can you refocus your everyday life to be more oriented towards this calling?

Heavenly Father, you are the ultimate Father. Please forgive me for the times I have not lived up to the dignity of fatherhood. Forgive my father for his shortcomings as well. Help all of us to embrace the responsibility to raise children according to your holy will and to teach them your ways. Grant me the grace to be an example to my children through my actions each day. Above all, create in me a heart to always provide a source of unconditional love for them.

St. Joseph, reveal to me Christ's hidden face present in my children. Teach me to manifest for them the Father who is rich in mercy. Amen.

Day 16

Honor Your Father and Mother

It can be intriguing to ponder the inner workings and interactions of the Holy Family. The first family member in the line-up is the Word Incarnate, the Second Person of the Blessed Trinity in the flesh. Then, there is the Blessed Virgin Mary, who was immaculately conceived and sinless. She embodies the masterpiece of the Father's creation and is entirely full of grace. Finally, there is St. Joseph, who was a simple carpenter and a man who spoke not a word in the Scriptures.

In this unique family, who was in charge? Who was teaching whom? Is it possible for humans to tell the Christ, the God-Man, what to do? Did they teach him how to do things, when to do things, how to treat people and how to put on sandals? Did his father teach him how to cut and handle wood? Was the Co-Creator of the Universe, who was there in the beginning with God, taught how to craft a table and chair with his own hands? These questions evoke great mysteries worth spending generous time contemplating, even if we cannot definitively come up with precise answers.

We learn from Scripture that "Jesus increased in wisdom and in stature, and in favor with God and man" (Luke 2:53). Jesus grew in his understanding of the world and his mission as he developed in age. Jesus was the most perfect version of a three year old, but he grew into the most perfect version of a four year old …and so on. In his humanity, he developed from perfection to perfection.

We can also presume that Jesus perfectly fulfilled the Commandments. Therefore, he honored his father and mother more perfectly than any child ever has or ever will. As St. Luke tells us, "he went down with [Mary and Joseph] and came to Nazareth, and was obedient to them" (Luke 2:51).

If this is true, what can we learn about St. Joseph as a father? How could Jesus have never sinned and always followed the will of the Heavenly Father, while still remaining obedient to his earthly father? The only reasonable explanation is that Joseph must have never asked anything of Jesus that was contrary or in opposition to God's will. Joseph was so in touch with the will of God the Father that he himself never led Jesus astray... ever. God the Father knew he could choose and entrust Joseph with this unique mission.

Personal Reflection:

Are we single-minded in raising our children in the ways of the Lord? When we teach our children how to make decisions, do we teach them to ask God what he desires and to consider his will for their path? Do we seek God's will in their choice of friends, in what school they should attend, for which charities they should serve, whom they should date, how they should spend their money, what media they consume, how many siblings they should have and so on? The most important and practical thing we can do in our lives is to follow the will of God. Do we lead our children with this same perspective, or do we simply shelter them from any discomfort that may come their way? Seek the intercession of St. Joseph in raising your children. Ask that he may reveal his wisdom to you so that you may grow in wisdom, knowledge and virtue as an individual and a parent.

Heavenly Father, since you commanded my children to honor me, encourage me to become a more honorable man. Stand by me as I discern your holy will in my own life so that I may guide those entrusted to me in your ways. Let me never lead them astray. Amen.

St. Joseph, reveal to me Christ's hidden face present in my children. Teach me to manifest for them the Father who is rich in mercy. Amen.

7 - 4 Sunday

Day 17

Anxiety

There are times in life when everything seems right and perfect, and other times when we feel completely lost and don't even know why. We experience those moments when our faith is strong, and feel as if we could handle anything that comes our way. Just when things get into a groove, our faith then falters, and we feel weak and frail. The human soul goes through many seasons in the journey to eternal life. The good news is that the God who created us knows and understands our human condition and frailty even better than we do. Our God is meek and humble and thirsts for our hearts and souls in every season, good or bad. God always desires to be near us regardless of our sin and lack of faith. In the midst of our anxiety, Christ wishes to meet us right where we are and bring us peace.

It may be comforting to know that Scripture tells us of a time when St. Joseph experienced anxiety. When Jesus was 12 years old, Mary and Joseph realized that they had left him behind in the Temple. Only afterwards do we hear relief in Mary's voice once they finally found him, "Behold, your father and I have been looking for you anxiously" (Luke 2:48).

This story is more than a testament of Mary and Joseph's humanity. It is a simple yet fundamental lesson for us all: **They were both anxious precisely when they lost Jesus!** The disappearance of Jesus at the Temple and the subsequent anxiety that followed illustrates undoubtedly what happens to the rest of us in our own spiritual lives. When we lose sight of Jesus and all of our worries and distractions get in the way, our vision becomes unclear. Where is Jesus in the midst of all the distractions?

As the author of the famous poem *Footprints in the Sand* contemplated, is it Jesus that deserts us in our time of need, or is it we that lose sight of him in those times when we need him the most? Discovering Jesus' presence ensures that he will restore peace once again in our lives. Fortunately, this story gives both the Holy Family and all of us the key to where to find him: at the Temple. As

Jesus said to them, "Why were you looking for me? Did you not know that I must be in my Father's house?" (Luke 2:49)

Personal Reflection

When do you most often fall into anxiety, and what are the main causes?

When you find yourself anxious and distressed, ask the Lord to come to your assistance. Ask him to show you his hidden face right in the midst of your crisis and fears. The Lord wishes to make himself known to you in the midst of any struggle you are going through, and he will be by your side through it all. Life will not be without burdens, struggles, disappointments, tragedy, loss and eventually even death, but our God promises that we do not have to endure these things alone.

When you come to these moments in life and are looking for a sign that God is real, cares for you and loves you, remember what Mary and Joseph had to do to relieve their anxiety. They had to find Jesus. They did not give into despair when they realized that they were the ones that left him behind, but instead they sought after him. Seek him and you will find him. In your pain, find him in his. Contemplate the scourging, the crown of thorns placed upon his head, the nails through his hands and feet, and the sword that pierced his heart. His heart was opened that you might receive his infinite love and mercy that flows without limits. When you are looking for a sign of the Father's love for you, gaze upon the cross and remember that there is no greater love. When the troubles of life become so great that your heart is completely open before God, and you find yourself begging and asking if everything will be "okay", gaze upon the cross and recall how the story ends. God brings a greater good. Easter Resurrection will come! Trust in the Lord.

What are some things you can do when the trials of life come your way so that the next time you will quickly turn to Jesus?

Heavenly Father, help me to trust in you with all that I am. Be near me especially in times of great anxiety. Bring clarity to me in these moments, Lord. I place my life in your hands and trust in your goodness. Bring me peace when I am troubled. Come to my aid. Seek after me when I lose sight of you. Forgive me for the times that I cannot find you because I have placed things in front of you that block my vision. Open my eyes Lord, as I want to see your face. Help me know that you are near.

St. Joseph, reveal to me Christ's hidden face present in my children. Teach me to manifest for them the Father who is rich in mercy. Amen.

Day 18

The Revelation of the Father

"Show us the Father and that shall be enough for us" (John 14:8).

The Apostle Philip professed these words to Christ in the Upper Room during the Last Supper. Apparently something in Philip's heart was not satisfied. Christ rebuked him saying, "Have I been with you so long, and yet you do not know me, Philip? He who has seen me has seen the Father" (John 14:9).

Philip did not fully understand that Jesus Christ himself was the Revelation of the Father. Nonetheless, Philip teaches us an invaluable lesson that the ultimate desire of the human heart is to be with God our Father, to glimpse the face of God and live. St. Augustine reaffirms this reality that resides in all of us, "Our hearts are restless until they rest in thee." To put this in perspective, Philip had previously witnessed the multiplication of the loaves, a blind man receiving sight, a paralyzed man rise up and walk, the calming of a storm, his friend Peter walk on water and even a dead man raised to life. What more could Philip possibly have wanted to see?

The desire to see the Father is a universal truth written into our hearts. The human heart thirsts for union with the infinite God, the source of life, love and superabundant mercy, and therefore cannot be fully satisfied with anything less. This perpetual yearning is part of the poverty we must face during our journey back to the Father.

When you consider these truths, the words of St. John Paul II come alive in a profound way when he says, "In revealing and in reliving on earth the very fatherhood of God, a man is called upon to ensure the harmonious and united development of all the members of the family" (Pope John Paul II, Familiaris Consortio, #25).

Wow! What dignity! What responsibility! What a noble and meaningful calling and vocation to which we all can strive!

Amazingly, by this definition, Joseph had the singular dignity to relive and reveal on Earth the very fatherhood of God to Jesus himself. God hand-picked Joseph for this vocation. Therefore, when the Christ-child looked up in admiration at his earthly father, he saw a man who was rich in mercy and love. Jesus saw a man who constantly poured himself out in sacrifice for the good of others. Second only to Jesus Himself, Joseph lived the words of St. John Paul II more fully and completely than any other man in history.

Personal Reflection:

Joseph was chosen by God for Jesus. Correspondingly, you were chosen by God for your children (or future children). You are called to become the revelation of the Father. When your children see you, they should see a man so entirely in love with God the Father that you manifest his love. They must see a man who regularly receives the mercy of God himself, so that you may manifest his mercy to others.

Unfortunately, many men have a wounded image of God because of the shortcomings of their own earthly father. Countless fathers have fouled up their fatherly vocation and fall short of this description of fatherhood. If your earthly father has wounded your image of God, draw closer to St. Joseph, who will point you in the direction of your Father in heaven. He will also lead you to his Son, the ultimate revelation of the Father.

Heavenly Father, my heart is restless until it rests in you. You are my ultimate desire. Help me never to settle for anything less. Instill a hunger in me to draw closer to you so that I may be filled with your love and mercy. Your grace is sufficient, Lord. **You are enough.** Amen.

St. Joseph, reveal to me Christ's hidden face present in my children. Teach me to manifest for them the Father who is rich in mercy. Amen.

Day 19

St. Joseph the Worker

My best friend from college used to affectionately reminisce about a daily conversation he frequently had with his father: "How was work today, Dad?" "Work is work, Johnny boy. That's why they call it work!"

Work is tedious. Work is a grind. It is hard, long and incredibly laborious. Work is work. At times however, work can also be extremely satisfying. Accomplishing something good, worthwhile and beneficial for others can lead to a gratifying sense of purpose and fulfillment. Through all of the peaks and valleys, one thing is for certain – we can work all day, all week and all year long, but there will always be more that we feel we must get done.

When it comes to labor, we need a patron. Thankfully, the Church points us to our good friend and companion, St. Joseph! The Liturgical Calendar recognizes St. Joseph specifically on two different feast days. The first is the Feast of St. Joseph as the Husband of Mary (March 19), and the other is the Feast of St. Joseph the Worker (May 1). How sweet it is to know that we don't have to toil alone. It is this faithful friend who can inspire us when we need motivation, carry us when we can't find the energy and remind us of our mission when we forget what it's all for.

There are certainly moments or even days when we wish we no longer had to work. Sometimes we dream that in a perfect world we could just hang up our bootstraps and chill out in relaxation for the rest of our lives. Is that true? If Adam and Eve had never succumbed to the forbidden fruit, would humanity enjoy perpetual R&R as we leisurely stroll through a life of bliss?

Contrary to popular belief, work has been an integral part of God's plan for humanity from the very beginning. Before sin entered the world Adam was already called to till the soil. Adam, made in the image and likeness of God, was called to work. The fundamental difference was that Adam's work was not laborious in nature, and it was always fruitful. After the Fall, Adam was forced to toil by the sweat of his brow and experience thorns and thistles (Cf.

Genesis 3:17-18). Work became difficult and was no longer always abundant with fruit.

Amidst the daily grind, we become like God in very tangible ways. First, God allows us to be creative. The Lord is the Creator of the universe, and yet he has given humanity the dignity to participate in his creative genius through our own human creativity. Second, God is the Provider. Through our work, humanity is given the dignity to provide for others as well. This is first and foremost lived out in our homes and our families. We are called by God to selflessly provide for the needs of our loved ones, both big and small. Scripture goes so far as saying, "If any one does not provide for his relatives, and especially for his own family, he has disowned the faith and is worse than an unbeliever" (1 Timothy 5:8). Consecrate your work to the Lord, and he will cultivate it to bear great fruit. The results may not always be what we expected, but God will be faithful when we entrust our lives and our work to him.

Personal Reflection:

In modern American culture, most noble, hard working men do not have a problem with making the daily sacrifices necessary, in order to take care of their families. Rather, more men today are wrestling with the pressure and temptation to overwork, all veiled under the slogans so commonly known as "Ambition", "Winning" and "Success". For many, the temptation is so great that they rarely ever see or relate to their families. Blindly, we sometimes believe that the more money we make, the better we can take care of our families. But when work and family collide and the balance begins to unravel, **the cost of our absence from our families outweighs the benefits** and in some cases, the damage has been done and cannot easily be reversed.

Consider St. Joseph. He was a carpenter by trade, and let's safely assume he was a very good carpenter. If Joseph thought like a modern-day American and understood that in order to take care of his family, he needed to grow his business as much as possible and make as much money as he could; what should he have done? Was it a wise decision to have moved to Nazareth? Can anything good come out of Nazareth (Cf. John 1:46)? Nazareth was by no means the mecca for business nor did it have a robust economy. Let me help you out, Joseph, with a little practical advice for your trade:

move to Jerusalem. More people, more work, more money to be made, and therefore more success. Joseph, don't you know you need to provide for your family?

Joseph moved to Nazareth because he listened to the voice of God. The Lord was his guide in all things including his practical business decisions, even if it affected his earning potential. Living in Nazareth was precisely what was needed for the protection and support of the Holy Family.

Having success and building wealth is not a bad thing, so long as we never lose focus on what is most important and we unwaveringly follow God's desires for our lives.

- Do you perform honest and noble work in order to support your family?
- Do you make it home to have dinner with your family at least five days a week?
- While you are at the dinner table with your family, do you check work emails, text messages and/or phone calls?
- After a long day's work, do you waste potentially valuable and precious time with your family on TV and/or other social media?

Heavenly Father, inspire me to emulate and consecrate all my work to you through St. Joseph.

St. Joseph, reveal to me Christ's hidden face present in my children. Teach me to manifest for them the Father who is rich in mercy. Amen.

Day 20

The Second Greatest Saint in Heaven

You were made for one purpose: to be a saint. For many of us, this may evoke a sense of doubt and disbelief. We raise the white flag in our hearts and believe that we are not good enough. In our minds, the saints represent a super-holy, select group of people that tower so highly above us that we can hardly make sense of or relate to. Some of their virtues and accomplishments seem so lofty that we are prone to dismiss them as mere ideals that are unpractical for our own lives. If you feel this way, welcome to the club! If you struggle with the weight of your own sinfulness, fears, insecurities and shortcomings, welcome to the human race. You are not alone!

> Alas! I have always noticed that when I compared myself to the saints, there is between them and me the same difference that exists between a mountain whose summit is lost in the clouds and the obscure grain of sand trampled underfoot by passers-by. Instead of becoming discouraged, I said to myself; God cannot inspire unrealizable desires. I can, then, in spite of my littleness, aspire to holiness. It is impossible for me to grow up, and so I must bear with myself such as I am with all my imperfections. (St. Therese, *Story of a Soul*)

To be a saint, we often feel as though we must travel on mission trips selflessly serving the needs of others, or that this is a calling reserved only for a select number of holy priests and ministers. If only we did not have these jobs to do and have these families to take care of…then we would have time to be saints.

In the fullness of time, God found the greatest man on Earth who did whatever was asked of him, faithfully followed God's will, didn't have an enlarged ego, and was willing to lay down his life for others. With an instrument like this, God was able to give him the greatest mission he could possibly award…drum roll, please…to be a husband and father.

From what we know, the second greatest saint in history did not spend his days preaching around the globe. In fact, as we learned earlier, we have not a single word recorded of anything Joseph said. The second greatest saint in history was a father and a spouse. Notwithstanding his union with God, those two things defined St. Joseph more than anything else.

This is good news for us! It means that we can find holiness and sanctity directly in the context of our ordinary daily lives. Yes, even if your job is mindlessly mundane as you do the exact same thing for eight straight hours every day. You can still come home to your family with joy in your heart, eager to spend the next several hours playing with and taking care of your children. When the day is finally over, entrust it all to the Lord and appeal to him to provide you with the energy to do it again tomorrow. This is the great challenge that lies before us. We can become great saints if we desire it! The daily demands of life and family provide all the obstacles and challenges we need to be men of great virtue and sanctity.

St. Joseph became a great saint because his heart was filled with love, and love is precisely what passes through the grave into everlasting life. **The family is where we first learn to love, and it can therefore be called the school of love.** Love makes saints because love makes it way to heaven. To make it to heaven is to be a saint!

Love is patient. Love is kind. Love endures all things. Love is not self-seeking but is always at the service of others (Cf. 1 Corinthians 13:4-8). This defined the life of St. Joseph. He placed the needs of his wife and his son above his own. Why was Joseph so hidden? How could this obscure historical figure become the second greatest saint of all? As he lived his life completely for others, Joseph became smaller and smaller and his hiddenness "grew". The wisdom of the Scriptures reveals this great paradox, "whoever would be great among you must be your servant, and whoever would be first among you must be slave to all" (Mark 10:43).

Personal Reflection:

In Scripture, Joseph disappeared so that the glory of God would shine forth. Joseph did not need glory but offered his life for the greater glory of God. As St. John the Baptist boldly proclaimed, "He must increase, but I must decrease" (John 3: 30). St. Paul said it another way, "It is no longer I who live, but Christ who lives in me" (Galatians 2:20). The Jesuits founded an entire order on this maxim: *AMDG* (All for the Greater Glory of God).

- Where do you place all of your energy and effort in your life?
- Do you work for the greater glory of God or for other reasons?
- What drives you?
- In what ways can you decrease so that the Lord may increase?
- In what ways can you grow in holiness and become more saint-like in the context of your everyday life?
- What is holding you back?

Every generation has its saints. God is calling you.

Heavenly Father, place in me the desire to desire you more. A desire to become a saint right in the midst my everyday life. Help me experience your love and joy more abundantly so that I may bring joy to those around me. Open my heart and mind to learn from the example of St. Joseph. Amen.

St. Joseph, reveal to me Christ's hidden face present in my children. Teach me to manifest for them the Father who is rich in mercy. Amen.

Day 21

Can anything good come out of Nazareth?

"Philip found Nathanael, and said to him, 'We have found him of whom Moses in the law and also the prophets wrote, Jesus of Nazareth, the son of Joseph.'

Nathanael said to him, 'Can anything good come out of Nazareth?'

Philip said to him, 'Come and see.'" John 1: 45-46

Philip's heart overflowed with excitement as he shared his joy with Nathanael. At that moment, he could have told him all about Jesus, but at the end of day, Philip knew that Nathanael had to experience Jesus for himself. He invited Nathanael into this relationship with Jesus Christ with three simple words, "Come and see."

This week, we enter into the School of Nazareth, and St. Joseph will be our host and guide to "come and see" the beauties and mystery of their home. Our goal will be to become acquainted with the inner workings of the Holy Family by peering into the lives they lived together. I believe that this is much more than an informational history lesson. We can truly enter into a spiritual relationship with Jesus Christ and the saints in heaven as they share with us the secrets of virtue and sanctity. Although it is mysterious and hidden, let us enter prayerfully into the School of Nazareth.

Personal Reflection:

Philip's simple invitation, "Come and see," contains more anticipation and promise than any words that I could ever write. Words can be an effective tool for an inspiring invitation, but nothing can replace a personal encounter. Your own experience of the Holy Family will be much more powerful and real than any explanation that I can give. In order for this to occur, you must enter more deeply into a relationship with Jesus, Mary and Joseph. This week, I invite you to deepen these relationships and ask the Lord to open your eyes and heart to the mystery of the Holy Family.

Nathanael was persuaded by Philip to meet Jesus, and we know from Scripture that it lived up to the hype. "Rabbi, you are the Son of God! You are the King of Israel" (John 1:49).

I have no doubt that if you earnestly seek to meet the Holy Family and join in the School of Nazareth, you will find a treasure.

Heavenly Father, aid us as we enter into the mystery of the Holy Family this week. Help us to learn whatever you wish to teach us. Give us the grace to make our families holy. Encourage us to never "judge a book by its cover" or judge other people by their appearance, race or gender. Comfort us to trust that you can and will bring good out of the least likely of places, just as you did at Nazareth, to Nathanael's dismay.

St. Joseph, reveal to me Christ's hidden face present in my children. Teach me to manifest for them the Father who is rich in mercy. Amen.

Section 5:

The School of Nazareth

"The word of God presents the family as the first school of wisdom, a school which trains its members in the practice of those virtues which make for authentic happiness and lasting fulfillment."
Pope Benedict XVI Homily, Mass at Nazareth, May 14, 2009

"Nazareth is a kind of school where we may begin to discover what Christ's life was like and even to understand his Gospel ... Here everything speaks to us, everything has meaning ... How I would like to return to my childhood and attend the simple yet profound school that is Nazareth!"
Pope Paul VI, Address at the Basilica of the Annunciation, January 5, 1964

Fri
7-9-21

Day 22

Joseph the Warrior

All of us have heard the phrase, "Nice guys finish last." There is this idea in the world today that "Meekness equals weakness," and humility so often implied that you will get walked on. Unfortunately, in many cases the meek and the humble do very well go unnoticed in their accomplishments and may not get the same attention, job opportunities or as many "likes" on their latest social media sites. Instead of encouraging men to be meek and humble, the world teaches men to go out into the world and dominate. We are encouraged to out-perform others so as to prove ourselves through our bank accounts, our possessions and our record of achievements. As someone once said, "Money is just a way of keeping score." Many men are totally dedicated to winning the game, as if life were a game to begin with.

Nevertheless, Christian men are called to be meek and humble. "Far from being weak, however, the meek possess an inner strength to restrain anger and discouragement in the midst of adversity" (*Ignatius Catholic Study Bible*). We can practice these ideals in the simple ways in which we respond to the challenges of everyday life. Whether our wives snap at us at the end of a long and frustrating day, or a guy rudely cuts us off on the freeway, our responses define us. It is inevitable that life will provide us with major adversities in which to practice these difficult virtues! How you respond to God's grace can truly make or break these experiences. We are called to be charitable, to love others and even pray for our enemies. It takes heroic strength and defining virtue!

Courage is also needed in order to withstand the storms of life that come our way. I can't help but call to mind one of my favorite speeches from the classic movie, *The Count of Monte Cristo*:

> Life is a storm my young friend, you will bask in the sunlight one moment, be shattered on the rocks the next. What makes you a man is what you do when that storm comes. You must look into the storm as you shout as you did in Rome. Do your worst for I will do mine. Then the

Fates will know you as we know you as Albert Mondego,
the man.

There is something compelling in a man that seems to be calling
us to fight and compete; but where is our ultimate battle? With
whom are we fighting?

Joseph is our ultimate example of what it means to live
authentic masculine Christianity. He was quite possibly the meekest
and most humble of all. Yet at the same time, he was without
question a warrior and a fighter. He participated in the greatest
battle of all time. However, it was precisely his humility and
meekness that allowed him to trample over the Evil One rather than
faltering before him.

St. John Paul II proclaimed, "The family is placed at the heart
of the great struggle between good and evil, between life and death,
between love and all that is opposed to love" (Letter to Families,
#23). Pope John Paul II insists that at the core and heart of Satan's
attack is the family. We see this vividly played out in the book of
Revelation. "And the dragon stood before the woman who was
about to bear a child, that he might devour her child when she
brought it forth; she brought forth a male child, one who is to rule
all the nations with a rod of iron, but her child was caught up to
God and to his throne" (Rev 12:4-5).

The Church understands this passage to have multiple
meanings, but it is particularly clear that evil is attacking Our Lady
and the Christ-child. This verse strikingly illustrates the attack of
Satan at the very heart of the family. This is both a **spiritual** and
a **practical** truth.

God chose Joseph for this battle because Joseph was a warrior
for God. When Joseph said "Yes" to take Mary as his bride and
Jesus as his Son, he was avowing "Yes" to engage in the most epic
battle in human history. He was prepared to fight to the end to keep
his family safe. From the beginning of Christ's life, the powers of
darkness wanted Joseph's child dead and were willing to go to
extreme lengths to accomplish their ambition. It's incredibly ironic
that Herod needed to take the life of an infant, the weakest and
most helpless of mankind, in order for him to remain in a position
of absolute power and strength. Herod represents an icon of what

men who desire power over humility are willing to do and what men of humility are up against.

On the other hand, Joseph was willing to do whatever the Lord asked of him no matter what the personal cost. What strength! Most men lack the strength because most men lack the meekness.

Personal Reflection:

Imagine that an intruder, or even worse, the Evil One himself, comes into your home every night while you are sleeping and slips directly into your children's room. He does not physically hurt them but instead tries to corrupt their minds and souls. He feeds them with lies and lust and anything else in opposition to God. Imagine now that he comes in through a subtle opening. He does not break in through the door or break the code from your alarm system. He is sly and cunning. He comes through your child's TV, his cell phone, her iPad and her computer. Like St. Joseph, are we protecting our children from the Evil One, or are we ignorantly inviting him in for easy and direct access?

Are we willing to fight for the souls of our children even when the battles seem increasingly difficult and unpractical in our eyes? We have been traveling with St. Joseph for quite some time now; what would he do? The technology we bring into our home is just one example. In what other scenarios do we need to stand strong?

Warriors don't fret or complain because they understand there is a monumental battle at hand; they are fighting against something bigger than themselves. Mary and Joseph resisted the lure to complain when they had nowhere to sleep the night of the birth of Jesus. How unpractical to take Mary into the middle of nowhere precisely when she was about to go into labor; but that is exactly what Joseph did!

- Are you prepared to fight for the souls of each and every member of your family?
- Are you willing to make spiritual sacrifices for them?
- Are you poised to be there for them in the toughest of times?

Heavenly Father, encourage me to get my priorities in order so that I may focus my attention on being a warrior for Christ and for my family. Strengthen me to fight the good fight of faith and stand firm as a guardian against evil for my own soul and those of my family. Illuminate my heart and mind so as to not get caught up in trying to impress the world or in gaining power and strength in the eyes of the world. My strength is in you. You alone are my rock and my fortress. Take my desire to battle and use it against the Evil One. Take my desire to compete and use it for your glory, O Lord. Make me a warrior for your kingdom.

St. Joseph, take me to Nazareth and train me in your ways. Help me to exclude all evil from my heart and my home. Amen.

Sat
7-11

Day 23

Good Morning, God

Occasionally our faith is so incredibly incarnational that it seems almost scandalous to think about. The beauty of God becoming man and walking the earth can almost seem too much to bear. Consider each morning in the home of the Holy Family. Joseph could wake up every morning and walk over to Jesus' room, open the door and say, "Good morning, God." The climax of human history is that our God became man and dwelt among us.

> To express ourselves in accordance with the paradox of the Incarnation we can certainly say that God gave himself a human face, the Face of Jesus, and consequently, from now on, if we truly want to know the Face of God, all we have to do is to contemplate the Face of Jesus! In his Face we truly see who God is and what he looks like! (Pope Benedict XVI, 6 September 2006)

The home in which Joseph lived was by definition a temple because God, the Word Incarnate, dwelt there! Joseph lived and breathed every day in the temple of his very home. Joseph went about his daily routine in the presence of God.

No man has gazed upon Christ with the love and affection of St. Joseph. His eyes have seen, ears have heard, hands have touched, arms have carried and heart has been set on fire by the glory of the Lord. Invite St. Joseph into your life so that he may help to set your heart on fire with the love of God and love for your children.

Personal Reflection

Close your eyes and imagine looking into the eyes of your child in the morning and saying, "Good morning, God." Reflect upon how that might transform your life and your home. Ponder to yourself if that knowledge would change the way your raise him or her.

You do not have to imagine any longer. Listen and contemplate deeply these words of Christ, "Whoever receives one such child in my name receives me" (Matthew 18:5).

If you have the eyes of faith, you are called to find the hidden face of Christ dwelling in your midst. If you have the ears to hear it, at times you are even called to hear God speak to you through your children. Like the Holy Family, your home is called to be a temple where the Lord dwells, the domestic church. Like the Holy Family, even if perhaps more hidden, you can truly find the face of God in your midst.

I believe we all understand that our children are not God Incarnate, but in a mystical yet real way Jesus Christ still resides hidden within them. The more you contemplate it, the more you will discover this awesome mystery. The more you discover the mystery, the more your life and your home will be transformed. It is the home that will renew the world. "The future of the world and of the Church passes through the family" (John Paul II, Familiaris Consortio).

Recalling our contemplation from yesterday, it is no wonder John Paul II could give us such a simple 'program' to follow. With St. Joseph as your guide, set out with renewed hope seeking the hidden face of Christ in your midst.

If you are not yet married with children, you can still seek the hidden face of Christ in others. Blessed Mother Teresa founded an entire religious order on this principle and spent her entire life doing so. She found that within the poorest of the poor dwelt the hidden face of Jesus, resonating the words spoken from Christ, "Whatsoever you do to the least of my people, that you do unto me" (Matthew 25:40).

Christ awaits us in others. Seek and you will find him.

Heavenly Father, open my eyes that I may find your hidden face dwelling in others, especially my wife and children. Inspire me to learn from St. Joseph and from the marvelous mysteries of the life of the Holy Family. Help me to make my heart and my home a worthy sanctuary for you. Come dwell within me, O Lord. "Better is one day in your courts than a thousand elsewhere" (Psalm 84:10).

St. Joseph, take me to Nazareth and train me in your ways. Help me to exclude all evil from my heart and my home. Amen.

Day 24

Two Turtle Doves

Often times, the decisions of the people in the Old Testament honestly leave me baffled. The story that gets me every time is the account of the Israelites building the golden calf to worship (Cf. Exodus 32:3-8). Seriously? They waited for years while begging for God to set them free from the bondage of the Pharaoh in Egypt. God liberated his people in dramatic fashion with plagues, miracles and the parting of the Red Sea, and yet they respond by building a senseless idol? Can humanity really choose lowly idolatry after they have seen the hand of God in action? In modern times, do we as Christians even run the risk of falling into idolatry? I think it is safe to say that we have aligned with the Israelites in choosing "idols" over God at times in our lives.

"Put to death therefore what is earthly in you: fornication, impurity, passion, evil desire, and covetousness, which is idolatry" (Colossians 3:5). Scripture equates covetousness, which is another word for greed, with idolatry. In fact, anything we place above God in our hearts and minds can become an idol, even if it can be construed as a good thing. Nonetheless, Scripture places a bone-chilling emphasis on money as highlighted in the following verses:

No one can serve two masters; for either he will hate the one and love the other, or he will be devoted to the one and despise the other. You cannot serve God and mammon. (Matthew 6:24)

The eye of the covetous man is insatiable in his portion of iniquity: he will not be satisfied till he consumes his own soul. (Sirach 14:9)

The love of money is the root of all evil. (1 Tim 6:10)

It is safe to say that, in our culture, many people love money with greater emphasis and intensity than they love God. Once again, humanity has found another golden calf to worship. Unfortunately, this obsession with money has crept into most of our lives in one way or another. When you swim in the ocean, you start to smell like fish!

We impulsively think that money will bring happiness, peace and security. We assume that money will solve our problems and help us to do God's work better. If we could just find a little more money!

When the Holy Family went to the temple once a year to offer their sacrifice, they offered a pair of turtledoves (Cf. Luke 2:24). This was the offering of a poor family (Cf. Leviticus 12:8). The Holy Family was not rich; rather, Jesus, Mary and Joseph were poor but not wanting. If you asked St. Joseph, he would tell you to substitute the name of Jesus for the word money in all of those beliefs. Jesus will bring you happiness. Jesus will bring your family peace and security. Jesus will solve all your problems. Jesus will help you to do God's work better. If you could just get a little more Jesus!

It is certainly true that we have to work hard to earn money because we need food, shelter, and other essentials to provide for ourselves and our families. In reality, money itself is neither good nor bad. How we make it, how we spend it and how we place the notion of money in our hearts are of greater concern. I've heard it said, "You can have money, you just can't let money have you."

At the School of Nazareth the poverty of the Holy Family teaches us that money is not our ultimate answer. The wisest, most fruitful, most blessed and most inspiring family in human history did not have a large bank account and significant net worth. They were content with what they had. They had Jesus.

Personal Reflection:

Do you have an insatiable desire for wealth and material possessions? Do you worry more about your financial state or your spiritual state of life?

> And he said to them, "Take heed, and beware of all covetousness; for a man's life does not consist in the abundance of his possessions ... he who lays up treasure for himself, and is not rich toward God." And he said to

his disciples, "Therefore I tell you, do not be anxious about your life, what you shall eat, nor about your body, what you shall put on. For life is more than food, and the body more than clothing. Consider the ravens: they neither sow nor reap, they have neither storehouse nor barn, and yet God feeds them. Of how much more value are you than the birds! And which of you by being anxious can add a cubit to his span of life? If then you are not able to do as small a thing as that, why are you anxious about the rest? Consider the lilies, how they grow; they neither toil nor spin; yet I tell you, even Solomon in all his glory was not arrayed like one of these. But if God so clothes the grass which is alive in the field today and tomorrow is thrown into the oven, how much more will he clothe you, O men of little faith! And do not seek what you are to eat and what you are to drink, nor be of anxious mind. For all the nations of the world seek these things; and your Father knows that you need them. Instead, seek his kingdom, and these things shall be yours as well. Fear not, little flock, for it is your Father's good pleasure to give you the kingdom. Sell your possessions, and give alms; provide yourselves with purses that do not grow old, with a treasure in the heavens that does not fail, where no thief approaches and no moth destroys. For where your treasure is, there will your heart be also." (Luke 12: 15 – 34)

Heavenly Father, have mercy on us when we place worldly things in front of you. Increase our faith in order to trust in your fatherly care for our needs. Help us to learn from St. Joseph that if we have Jesus, we have enough. Give us this day our daily bread. Support us as we provide sufficiently for our families. If we have surplus, teach us to use it according to your holy will.

St. Joseph, take me to Nazareth and train me in your ways. Help me to exclude all evil from my heart and my home. Amen.

Day 25

The Program of Saint John Paul II

At the turn of the millennium, we find a world that has become increasingly secularized, yet amidst the darkness there remains great hope. Saint John Paul II led us into this new era with a culture he described as "a culture of death." However, the Holy Father was also the one whose hope remained firm as he spoke of a "new springtime for Christianity."

How do we combat the evils of our times? We experience wars, abortions, morality issues, justifications of sin of every sort, threatened religious liberties, attacks on the institution of marriage, the rise of atheism and agnosticism and the explosion of pornography. The list could go on. What gives? What are we to do? What is our plan?

Fully aware of the evil at hand, John Paul II had the boldness to speak of hope as he presented Christians with an earth-shattering plan. "To contemplate the face of Christ, and to contemplate it with Mary, is the 'programme' which I have set before the Church at the dawn of the third millennium, summoning her to put out into the deep on the sea of history with the enthusiasm of the new evangelization" (Pope John Paul II, *Ecclesia de Eucaristia*, #6).

At the heart of the matter, the Holy Father pointed us back in simplicity to the Way, the Truth, and the Life; namely Jesus Christ. The world's problems are solved in a heartfelt return to the face of Jesus Christ. The statement above also shows us quite simply why the world is experiencing such difficult times and massive evil, precisely because it has turned away from the face of Christ. When we turn from the Lord, everything unravels and evil gets a foot in the door. When we turn from the Lord, we are left to ourselves and our firm foundations turn to sand. As such, we cannot weather the storms of time alone. When we turn from the face of Christ, the Evil One outsmarts us every time. Every sin becomes justifiable in our eyes. We settle for comforts and creatures rather than the love of the Creator. In essence, when we turn from the face of Christ, we become lost. Lost in the culture, lost in our own humanity and lost in our journey to eternal life.

The Holy Father provides the simplest of solutions: contemplate Christ. When we contemplate Christ, we find love, not love that we find in the modern world, but divine love. "Merely to look upon the crucified God is to begin to understand that what passes for human love is often nothing more than a front for the sheer egoism of the self-centered self" (Regis Martin, *Still Point*). Christ teaches us the meaning of life. His sacrifice on the cross can't help but remind us of sin and the human condition. It reminds us that we need a Savior.

The second aspect of the "program" that Pope John Paul II left with us challenges us to contemplate the face of Christ with Mary. Why? Because Mary knew Christ the best! She always contemplated the mysteries of Christ in her heart (Cf. Luke 2:19). Her heart was more closely united to the heart of Christ than any other heart. She was there when he was conceived. She was there when he was born. She was there when he started his public ministry. She was there when he emptied himself upon the cross. She witnessed the Resurrected Christ not only as a bystander, but also as a mother. She was there at Pentecost for the gift of the Holy Spirit. And she was there for thirty years of his hidden life in Nazareth. Who could possibly be a better model and companion for us as we contemplate the face of Christ?

Who first contemplated the face of Christ with Mary? You guessed it – Joseph. St. Joseph most perfectly lived these words. He was the first to gaze upon the Savior, to look into the eyes of love and mercy, to bring Christ into his heart and his home and to see the Word become flesh. There is no doubt that his mind was in constant contemplation through his everyday experiences. He witnessed all these things contemplatively with Mary at his side. Together, they entered into the greatest mystery of love the world has ever known. Through the Holy Family, Salvation himself entered into the world.

Another way to understand the 'program' put in place for this new millennium and new evangelization is to enter into the mystery of St. Joseph. He is hidden in Scripture and is even hidden in John Paul's statement. Although veiled in obscurity, he is present, and he is fruitful. Joseph once again teaches us a great lesson in humility. It's not about making sure you are known or making a statement in this world so that others may praise you, it's about being close to God and gazing upon his face. That is precisely when God can fully accomplish his will through you.

Personal Reflection

One of the most practical ways to contemplate the face of Christ with Mary is to contemplate the mysteries of Christ's life through the Rosary. Together with Our Lady, you draw deeper into the glorious story of our salvation filled with great sorrows, lasting joys and final victory. Consider incorporating the Rosary into your daily spiritual life and ask St. Joseph to be with you as you enter into the contemplation with Our Lady.

Heavenly Father, thank you for the gift of the Holy Family. Help me to enter more deeply into their life with Christ. Please forgive me for the times I have turned to the world for answers instead of gazing upon the face of Christ. As I seek his face today, I already experience the peace. Ease the doubts, fears and distractions in my life.

St. Joseph, take me to Nazareth and train me in your ways. Help me to exclude all evil from my heart and my home. Amen.

Day 26

Holy Death and Heroic Trust

We all have our greatest fear, and in vulnerability I will share mine with you today. As a husband and father of small children, I am afraid that I will pass from this world to the next too soon. As the old country song says, "Lord, I want to go to heaven I just don't want to go tonight" (Joe Diffie, *Prop Me Up Beside the Jukebox*). The fear is twofold. The obvious reason is that I love my family and cherish every second with them. I have loved every moment of every day during my daughters' first years. Sure, there may have been a few two year-old moments that I didn't love so much, but overall every age has brought singular blessings I have been able to joyfully hold on to. I want to see my daughters as six year olds, sixteen year olds and someday as adults with their own children. Moreover, I want to be there through all the struggles in life to teach them, guide them and love them every step of the way.

My second part of this fear is much more intense. I understand that heaven is far better than anything I could hope for or imagine, so while missing out on their lives seems terrifying, I believe in the promises of Christ. I can trust that somehow heaven will be even greater than this. Therefore, the greatest fear is the thought of my wife and children going through life without their husband and father. While I avoid spending my days in fear, I do pray to God for a long life.

Once again, we have an incredible lesson to learn from the life experience of St. Joseph. Through the tradition of the Church, we recognize that Joseph passed from this earth before the beginning of Jesus' public ministry. Many believe that Joseph lived with Jesus and Mary for thirty years. Thus we have a thirty day novena to St. Joseph, one day for each year he spent with Jesus and Mary. This idea helped influence this book as a thirty day journey. However long he spent with them, from a human perspective it was far from enough.

From the human relationship between a father and a son and between a husband and a wife it was not enough. Jesus began his public ministry without the presence of St. Joseph. Jesus had to go through the most challenging moments of his life, his bitter passion and death on the cross, without St. Joseph by his side. Mary, who had her loving husband to protect her for so long, had to go through her greatest suffering without him as well.

From a purely human perspective, the death of St. Joseph could appear to be a tragedy. Instead, we hear quite the opposite in Church tradition. The death of St. Joseph is known throughout the Church to have been a holy and peaceful death. If you have ever been to the Basilica of the Sacred Heart at the University of Notre Dame, there is a strikingly beautiful painting by Luigi Gregori of the death of St. Joseph with Jesus and Mary at his side. Peace in the midst of what may cause others distress. Peace in the midst of what I could call my deepest fear. How could there be such a superabundant peace in the death of this holy man who was leaving his wife and son behind?

Peace is a fruit brought about by the total abandonment and surrender to the will of God in our lives. Joseph had been through so many miracles in his life. He experienced the bountiful goodness and graciousness of God. Joseph fully trusted God with all of his mind, strength, heart and soul. Although Joseph could not continue to be present and available for his wife and son, he trusted once again in the goodness of God for them. He knew God had a plan. God chose Joseph as the guardian for the Holy Family during those thirty fateful years, but now God could accomplish his most holy will with Joseph alongside him in heaven.

The death of Joseph was not a crisis for Joseph, nor was it a crisis for Mary or Jesus. They knew he was a just man before God, a man after God's own heart, and that they would be with him once again for all eternity. This deep trust and unshakable faith resulted in a death that was full of peace. They may have felt sadness for their temporary time away from him, but borrowing from the Scriptures, "Perfect love casts out fear. For fear has to do with punishment, and he who fears is not perfected in love (1 John 4:18).

Personal Reflection

Today's reflection is less about death and more about trust. Trust in God drives out anxiety and fear. Joseph died in the arms of Jesus and Mary, and nothing could be more comforting at the hour of death. May we also rest in the loving arms of Jesus and Mary as we pass from this world to the next.

- Do you fully trust in the goodness of God for your life and the lives of your loved ones?
- Do you confide in the fact that God is an even better and more loving father than you are?

"Cast your worries upon him who cares for you" (1 Peter 5:7).

Heavenly Father, thank you for my life and the time that you have given me on this Earth. Thank you for the loved ones with whom you have filled my life. I repent of not trusting you with all my heart, of all my doubt and fears. Lord, you are all good and all merciful. Increase my faith and grant that I may walk in joy and peace all my days. It is for freedom that you have set me free. Give me the grace that I may not waste time in anxiety and fear. Jesus, I trust in you.

St. Joseph, take me to Nazareth and train me in your ways. Help me to exclude all evil from my heart and my home. Amen.

Day 27

Paradise

As a child growing up in the 90's there is no question that I listened to the Irish rock band, U2. For better or for worse, music is an incredibly powerful form of art. Decades later, I can still remember the lyrics to one of their hit songs, "I Still Haven't Found What I'm Looking For." This song is considered one of the greatest rock songs of all time for various reasons. In a sense, it resonates within people because deep down there is a universal truth that nothing will satisfy our hearts this side of heaven. Millions have sung along with Bono these very words, "I have climbed the highest mountains. I have run through the fields…but I still haven't found what I'm looking for."

Deep down in all of our hearts, God has placed a desire for the infinite. He has placed in us a desire to enter into paradise. Only then will we fully "find what we are looking for."

Before the fall, Adam and Eve experienced a type of paradise in the Garden of Eden. I had a theology professor in college who liked to speculate on how long it took Adam and Eve to sin. We may never know the real answer but his theory was, "About eight seconds."

When sin entered the world, paradise was lost. God placed an angel at the garden entrance with a flaming sword "to guard the way to the tree of life" (Genesis 3:24). Ever since, humanity has been toying with every pleasure under the sun to try and satisfy this desire in our hearts. Nothing seems to quench our thirst. On the other hand, God always had a plan to reopen the gates and bring us back to him.

Through some of the most beautiful theology you can imagine, the Church Fathers understood that at the moment of the wounding of Christ' heart, paradise was restored. "One of the soldiers pierced his side with a spear, and at once there came out blood and water" (John 19:34). The earthly soldier that pierced the heart of Christ with his lance reminds us of the angel that blocked paradise with his sword. We have access to paradise once more through the wounded heart of Christ.

There flowed from his side blood and water. Beloved, do
not pass over this mystery without thought; it has yet
another hidden meaning, which I will explain to you. I said
that the water and blood symbolized baptism and the Holy
Eucharist. From these two sacraments the Church is born.
(St. John Chrysostom, Office of Readings, Good Friday)

Christ's death on the cross, which is the new tree of life, and the
opening of his heart have paid our ransom for sin. From this
moment, the Church was born. As St. Augustine mystically made
known, "What then was Paradise is now represented by the
Church." From the new tree of life, we also have the new plentiful
fruit that sustains us: the Eucharist. Therefore in the Church, we
have direct access to paradise every Sunday, and possibly every day
for those of us extra thirsty souls.

Where did this fruit from the new tree of life come
from? "Blessed are you among women and blessed is the fruit of
your womb, Jesus" (Luke 1:42).

The fruit of the new tree of life dwelled in Mary for nine
months and subsequently in the home of Joseph and Mary for thirty
years. The Holy Family **was** paradise.

[The Holy Family] was a heaven, a paradise on earth,
endless delights in this place of grief; it was a glory already
begun in the vileness, abjection and lowliness of their life.
(Monsieur Jean-Jacques Olier, *The Shadow of the Father*)

Personal Reflection

How great is the longing in your heart for paradise? In what
ways do you try to quench that thirst with the things of this world?

Today, we discovered an answer to Bono's thirst as well as our
own. In the words of St. Augustine, "The Church becomes a well of
satisfaction by this gift of the Spirit ... for it is in her a fountain of
living water springing up unto everlasting life" (*The Writings Against
the Manichaens and the Donatists*).

Joseph and the Holy Family found this satisfaction, this
paradise, right in the midst of their home in Nazareth. The Holy
Family is the model and example of what God wishes for your

Christian home to become. God wishes for you to enter into the mystery of the School of Nazareth and learn at the side of St. Joseph. In what ways can you bring Christ more intimately into your home and everyday life?

Heavenly Father, my heart longs to enter into yours. Through the wounding of Christ's heart, your love for me has been poured out in abundance. Help me to bathe in your mercy and grace. Lead me as I find my way to paradise through the Sacred Heart of Jesus. And guide me to discover the mysteries of paradise on earth just as truly as did your servant, St. Joseph.

St. Joseph, take me to Nazareth and train me in your ways. Help me to exclude all evil from my heart and my home. Amen.

Section 6:

Conclusion

"St. Joseph's mission is certainly unique and unrepeatable, as Jesus is absolutely unique. However, in protecting Jesus, in teaching him how to grow in age, wisdom and grace, he is a model for every educator, and in particular for every father. ... I ask for you the grace to be ever closer to your children, allow them to grow, but be close, close! They need you, your presence, your closeness, your love. Be, for them, like St. Joseph: protectors of their growth in age, wisdom and grace. Guardians of their path, and educators: walk alongside them. And with this closeness, you will be true educators."

Pope Francis, General Audience, Solemnity of St. Joseph, March 19, 2014.

Day 28

Deeper Silence Still

Throughout this journey we have learned of the humility and silence of St. Joseph. As we approach the end of our journey, let us enter even more deeply into this mystery of silence.

Scripture:

We know that Scripture does not record a single spoken word from the mouth of St. Joseph, but let's take a look at the times he is at least mentioned. Of the 3,725 verses contained in the four Gospels, there are 40 that mention Joseph in some way. This count includes phrases such as "Son of the carpenter," which is the only way John refers to Joseph. Mark leaves Joseph out altogether. Matthew and Luke give us the most information we have about St. Joseph through the infancy narratives. In addition, Matthew records the dream of St. Joseph for us. It is wise to contemplate the few passages regarding St. Joseph and the greater message made apparent by our conclusion: Joseph is silent and hidden.

Church Fathers:

St. Joseph is virtually absent in the writings of the early Church Fathers. When he is mentioned, it is nearly always a reference to the fact that he guarded Mary's virginity or that he was the foster-father of Jesus. Conclusion: Joseph is silent and hidden.

Rome:

The four major churches in Rome are St. Peter's, St. Paul, Mary Major, and St. John Lateran (named for both John the Baptist and the Apostle John). The next most significant churches have nothing to do with Joseph either. No major church in Rome is named after St. Joseph. Conclusion: Joseph is silent and hidden.

Liturgy:

- 1479 – It took the Church over 1,400 years to officially make a universal feast day for St. Joseph. Pope Sixtus IV declared March 19 the universal Feast of St. Joseph.
- 1870 – It took almost 1,900 years before Pope Pius IX declared St. Joseph the Patron of the Universal Church.
- 1962 – It took over 19 centuries before Pope John XXIII inserted St. Joseph's name into the Roman Canon for the Eucharistic prayer. There were 24 saints named before him.

Conclusion: Joseph has been amazingly silent and hidden throughout the history of Church liturgy as well.

It is safe to say that over 2,000 years after the birth of Christ, St. Joseph continues to remain hidden in silence. **God speaks in the silence.** In order for us to progress in our understanding of St. Joseph, we must turn down the noise in our lives and enter into profound contemplation with him. If we do so, he will teach us the ways of God, the will of God and the adoration of God. He will teach us where to find God. He will teach us how to hear the voice of God and how to act upon it. He will teach us unfailing obedience, heroic trust, peace that surpasses all understanding, purity of heart, mercy that knows no bounds and a love that conquers the grave. Finally, he will invite us into his home and show us the secret delights of the Holy Family in Nazareth. Our journey is coming to an end, but yours with St. Joseph has really just begun!

Personal Reflection:

- In what ways can you create more silence in your life so that you may hear the voice of the Lord?
- In which areas of your daily life do you turn on the noise?

Heavenly Father, my journey with St. Joseph is ultimately a journey towards you. I seek to draw closer to you through your saints. Your light and your virtues have shown through them like the rays of sun through a stained glass window. Your beauty is made known through your saints, O Lord. Shine through me as well. Help me to become a light to the world by reflecting your light, O Lord.

Open my mind and my heart to the wisdom you wish to teach me through your son and servant, St. Joseph.

St. Joseph,
Mystery hidden from the wise and learned,
But revealed to little ones.
Take me to Nazareth and train me in your ways.
Reveal to me Christ's hidden face present in my children.
Unveil for me the love of the Holy Spirit present in my spouse.
Teach me to manifest for them the Father who is rich in mercy.
Help me to exclude all evil from my heart and my home,
So that we might find union with God,
And experience his love, peace and joy. Amen.
(Prayer written by Steve Bollman.)

Day 29

Recapping Our Journey

We have journeyed with St. Joseph for thirty days, and at last we have reached the end. That being said, hopefully this book is not the end of your pilgrimage as St. Joseph quietly waits to lead you to even greater spiritual heights.

We began this journey by reflecting upon the fact that God did not need Joseph to accomplish his plan for the salvation of the world, but that in his divine providence he chose him. This helped us understand that God has chosen us as well for a specific vocation. Like St. Joseph, God has chosen us to be a constant source of love for those near to us.

Next, we reflected on the silence and hiddenness of St. Joseph and the fact that we do not have a single spoken word from him in all of Scripture. We learned that his silence and obscurity speaks volumes to us. His profound humility before God paved the way for what would be asked of him. St. Joseph was a living example of the famous quote from St. Francis of Assisi, "Preach the gospel at all times, and when necessary use words." It proved unnecessary for St. Joseph to use words but instead to make way for the Word Incarnate, Jesus.

Then we considered the three main vocations, or missions, of St. Joseph. He was a just man before God, the spouse of Mary and the foster-father of Jesus. We reflected upon different aspects for each one of these most worthy missions.

Just Man Before God

St. Joseph was the ultimate "man after God's own heart" because he always did what the Lord asked. His obedience to the voice of God and the will of God was always instantaneous. He was willing to follow God's plan for him at all costs and even when it appeared to be far from practical at best. We learned that God seeks such men who are filled with humility and obedience, who trust in his providence, and who love him with their whole hearts to bear great fruit in the world. We asked the Lord to transform us into such men.

Spouse of Mary

Finding these amazing virtues in St. Joseph, God knew he had a suitable match for his most beautiful masterpiece, the one that was full of grace, our mother Mary. We learned that being the spouse of Mary was not for the faint of heart. Instead it was for the most pure of heart! To be the spouse of the Immaculata herself required heroic purity and sacrifice. From the very onset, from the moment of the Annunciation, things got interesting. Joseph was faced with an unprecedented situation and responded with a foreshadowing answer. He chose mercy. He was willing to destroy his reputation for her apparent shame and take it as if it were his own. God brought clarity to the situation through an angel and thirty-three years later offered his only Son instead to carry the burden of our shame. We asked the Lord to help us love our spouses the way St. Joseph did.

Father of Jesus

The ultimate mission of St. Joseph was to be the foster-father of Jesus. As men, we contemplated the profound quote from Saint John Paul II, "In revealing and in reliving on earth the very fatherhood of God, a man is called upon to ensure the harmonious and united development of all the members of the family" (Pope John Paul II, Familiaris Consortio, #25). By the nature of God's calling for him, Joseph became the revelation of God the Father to Jesus. "The admirable St. Joseph was given to the earth to express the adorable perfection of God the Father in a tangible way. In his person alone, he bore the beauties of God the Father ... one saint alone is destined to represent God the Father" (Fr. Andrew Doze, *The Shadow of the Father*). In short, we have to learn how to be not just good dads, but great dads. For better or for worse, our children will form part of their concept of God the Father through us, their earthly fathers. This dignity and responsibility as fathers is enormous, but the joys of living this out are indescribable. In our gift of self to our children, we begin to live the life of God. We become the hands and feet of the loving and merciful Father on the earth.

The School of Nazareth

If we have followed the path of Joseph in becoming men after God's own heart, developed into incredible spouses willing to sacrifice for our brides, and transformed into fathers who allow God's love and mercy to shine through us, our homes become nothing short of a type of paradise. We have allowed St. Joseph and the Holy Family to teach us their secrets at the School of Nazareth. Tomorrow, we take one final step.

Personal Reflection

Spend several minutes in silence reflecting on the pathway of St. Joseph and your own journey in the process. Take this opportunity to write down the spiritual insights that he has taught you along the way.

Heavenly Father, our journey with St. Joseph is ultimately a journey towards union with you. You are the one that we seek. You are the one for whom we long. St. Joseph was a just man after your own heart even before Christ came into the world. Therefore, you blessed him with the grace to see the face of God in Jesus Christ. God came to dwell in his home and be with him even here on the earth. Heavenly Father, come be with me. Come into my home. Reveal yourself to me. Open my eyes of faith so that I may see the revelation of your glory in my home. Help me to transform my home into a little Nazareth, a retreat from the world, a little paradise where you are present.

St. Joseph,
Mystery hidden from the wise and learned,
But revealed to little ones.
Take me to Nazareth and train me in your ways.
Reveal to me Christ's hidden face present in my children.
Unveil for me the love of the Holy Spirit present in my spouse.
Teach me to manifest for them the Father who is rich in mercy.
Help me to exclude all evil from my heart and my home,
So that we might find union with God,
And experience his love, peace and joy. Amen.
(Prayer written by Steve Bollman.)

Day 30

The School of Love

In heaven, all things are simplified, and only one thing remains-**Love!**

St. Joseph saw the face of God every day in his child. God dwelled in his midst and through this experience his heart was set on fire with love. Mary was overshadowed with the Holy Spirit, who St. Thomas Aquinas calls Love with a capital "L." Together, Mary and Joseph experienced love on earth in the most profound way.

The secret passage to love, to paradise, is an open door to the Sacred Heart of Christ. His heart was wounded and opened by a sword, so that ours may be healed. An infinite love flows perpetually from his heart. Love is the strongest power in both the world and the heavens. Yes, love is more powerful than even the grips of death. It transcends this life and passes to everlasting life in heaven. Our actions, when done in and through love, transcend this life and have everlasting significance. This is precisely why we can and should find paradise at the School of Nazareth. Quite simply, the daily life of the Holy Family was an explosion of love. When we find pure love and the absence of evil, we find paradise...even on earth.

St. Joseph has guided us throughout this journey and we have reached the end. He walked us through so many heroic virtues and taught us such invaluable wisdom along the way, but in the end he wishes to lead us to one thing- **Love.** Our hearts must be transformed in and through Love. When we receive the fullness of Divine Love into our own hearts, we receive that for which we were made, and we are transformed into a living flame of love. At this point, paradise doesn't seem so far away. Instead, you can enjoy a foretaste of paradise today.

Personal Reflection

How can you make your heart and your home a type of paradise? Some may be tempted to think this is only an ideal that cannot be practically lived. You may think that you have particular issues or circumstances in life that make this ideal impossible. Life brings crosses to each and every one of us. The Holy Family had their fair share of them as well. Moreover, they had The Cross. The Holy Family taught us how to love in the midst of suffering, in the midst of trials and in the midst of uncertainty.

Some may be tempted to question how this ideal of paradise in your heart and home can take place if your wife and children are not on board. Let's be honest, none of us have the Blessed Virgin Mary as our spouse, and none of us have Jesus Christ as our child. Regardless of your particular situation, the real question you should ask yourself is, "How can **I** enter more deeply into the mystery of love through the pierced heart of the Savior?"

Love conquers *all* things. When your heart becomes a living flame of love, you cannot force it upon others, and it does not guarantee their conversion, but you can offer it to anyone you encounter. If you reach this point, you have become a reflection of Christ and revelation of God the Father. You have climbed to the heights of sanctity with your most trusted friend, St. Joseph, to guide you every step of the way.

Heavenly Father, fill me at daybreak with your love, for your love is better than life itself. Show me a Father's love, and teach me to love as you have loved. Purge my heart of all but love, so that even now I may begin to taste the joys of paradise.

St. Joseph,
Mystery hidden from the wise and learned,
But revealed to little ones.
Take me to Nazareth and train me in your ways.
Reveal to me Christ's hidden face present in my children.
Unveil for me the love of the Holy Spirit present in my spouse.
Teach me to manifest for them the Father who is rich in mercy.
Help me to exclude all evil from my heart and my home,
So that we might find union with God,
And experience his love, peace and joy. Amen.
(Prayer written by Steve Bollman.)

Section 7:

Prayers for St. Joseph's Intercession

"Some Saints are privileged to extend to us their patronage with particular efficacy in certain needs, but not in others; but our holy patron St. Joseph has the power to assist us in all cases, in every necessity, in every undertaking."
St. Thomas Aquinas

Prayer of Entrustment to St. Joseph
By Steve Bollman

St. Joseph,

Mystery hidden from the wise and learned,

But revealed to little ones.

Take me to Nazareth and train me in your ways.

Reveal to me Christ's hidden face present in my children.

Unveil for me the love of the Holy Spirit present in my spouse.

Teach me to manifest for them the Father who is rich in mercy.

Help me to exclude all evil from my heart and my home,

So that we might find union with God,

And experience his love, peace and joy.

Amen.

Litany of St. Joseph

Lord, have mercy.	*Lord, have mercy.*
Christ, have mercy.	*Christ, have mercy.*
Lord, have mercy.	*Lord, have mercy.*
Jesus, hear us.	*Jesus, graciously hear us*
God, the Father of Heaven,	*Have mercy on us.*
God, the Son, Redeemer of the world,	*Have mercy on us.*
God, the Holy Spirit,	*Have mercy on us.*
Holy Trinity, One God,	*Have mercy on us*
Holy Mary,	*Pray for us.*
St. Joseph,	*Pray for us.*
Renowned offspring of David,	*Pray for us.*
Light of Patriarchs,	*Pray for us.*
Spouse of the Mother of God,	*Pray for us.*
Chaste guardian of the Virgin,	*Pray for us.*
Foster father of the Son of God,	*Pray for us.*
Diligent protector of Christ,	*Pray for us.*
Head of the Holy Family,	*Pray for us.*
Joseph most just,	*Pray for us.*
Joseph most chaste,	*Pray for us.*
Joseph most prudent,	*Pray for us.*
Joseph most strong,	*Pray for us.*
Joseph most obedient,	*Pray for us.*
Joseph most faithful,	*Pray for us.*
Mirror of patience,	*Pray for us.*
Lover of poverty,	*Pray for us.*
Model of artisans,	*Pray for us.*
Glory of home life,	*Pray for us.*
Guardian of virgins,	*Pray for us.*
Pillar of families,	*Pray for us.*
Solace of the wretched,	*Pray for us.*
Hope of the sick,	*Pray for us.*
Patron of the dying,	*Pray for us.*
Terror of demons,	*Pray for us.*
Protector of Holy Church,	*Pray for us.*

Litany of St. Joseph (continued)

Lamb of God, who take away the sins of the world,	*Spare us, O Lord.*
Lamb of God, who take away the sins of the world,	*Graciously hear us, O Lord.*
Lamb of God, who take away the sins of the world.	*Have mercy on us.*
He made him the lord of his household.	*And prince over all his possessions.*

Let us pray, O God, in your ineffable providence you were pleased to choose Blessed Joseph to be the spouse of your most holy Mother; grant, we beg you, that we may be worthy to have him for our intercessor in heaven whom on earth we venerate as our Protector: You who live and reign forever and ever.

Saint Joseph, pray for us.

First Century Prayer to St. Joseph

O St. Joseph, whose protection is so great, so strong, so prompt before the Throne of God, I place in you all my interests and desires.

O St. Joseph, do assist me by your powerful intercession and obtain for me from your Divine Son all spiritual blessings through Jesus Christ, Our Lord, so that having engaged here below your heavenly power I may offer my thanksgiving and homage to the most loving of Fathers. O St. Joseph, I never weary contemplating you and Jesus asleep in your arms. I dare not approach while He reposes near your heart. Press Him in my name and kiss His fine head for me, and ask Him to return the kiss when I draw my dying breath. St. Joseph, Patron of departing souls, pray for us. Amen.

Invocations to St. Joseph
By Father Olier

Hail Joseph, image of God the Father.
Hail Joseph, father of God the Son.
Hail Joseph, temple of the Holy Ghost.
Hail Joseph, beloved of the Holy Trinity.
Hail Joseph, most faithful helper in the great plan of Redemption.
Hail Joseph, most worthy spouse of the Virgin Mother.
Hail Joseph, father of all the faithful.
Hail Joseph, guardian of holy virgins.
Hail Joseph, greatest lover of poverty.
Hail Joseph, example of meekness and patience.
Hail Joseph, mirror of humility and obedience.

Blessed art thou among all men.
And blessed are thine eyes, which have seen what thou hast seen.
And blessed are thine ears, which have hears what thou hast heard.
And blessed are thy hands, which have touched the Word Incarnate.
And blessed are thine arms, which have carried the One Who carries all things.
And blessed is thy breast, on which the Son of God most sweetly reposed.
And blessed is thy heart, kindled with most ardent love.
And blessed be the Eternal Father, Who chose thee.
And blessed be the Son, Who loved thee.
And blessed be the Holy Ghost, Who sanctified thee.
And blessed be Mary, thy spouse, who loved thee as a spouse and a brother.
And blessed be the Angel who guarded thee.
And blessed be forever all who bless thee and who love thee.

Prayer for Purity

O GUARDIAN of Virgins and holy Father St. Joseph, into whose faithful keeping were entrusted Christ Jesus, Innocence itself, and Mary, Virgin of virgins, I pray and beseech thee by these dear pledges, Jesus and Mary, that, being preserved from all uncleanness, I may with spotless mind, pure heart and chaste body, ever serve Jesus and Mary most chastely all the days of my life. Amen.

Grant us, dear Joseph, to run life's pathway in innocent fashion:
May we be ever safe under thy blest patronage.

O Saint Joseph, foster-father of our Lord Jesus Christ and true spouse of Mary the Virgin, pray for us.

Prayer for Workers

Glorious St. Joseph, model of all who are devoted to labor, obtain for me the grace to work in the spirit of penance in expiating for my sins; to work conscientiously by placing love of duty above my inclinations; to gratefully and joyously deem it an honor to employ and to develop by labor the gifts I have received from God; to work methodically, peacefully and in moderation and patience, without ever shrinking from it through weariness or difficulty.

Above all, with purity of intention and unselfishness, having unceasingly before my eyes death and the account I have to render of time lost, talents unused, good not done, and vain complacency in success, so baneful to the work of God.

All for Jesus, all for Mary, all to imitate thee, O patriarch St. Joseph! This shall be my motto for life and eternity. Amen.

Prayer to the Holy Family
By Pope Francis

Jesus, Mary and Joseph, in you we contemplate the splendor of true love, to you we turn with trust.

Holy Family of Nazareth, grant that our families too may be places of communion and prayer, authentic schools of the Gospel and small domestic Churches.

Holy Family of Nazareth, may families never again experience violence, rejection and division: may all who have been hurt or scandalized find ready comfort and healing.

Jesus, Mary and Joseph, graciously hear our prayer. Amen.

PARADISUS DEI®